Cookies
& Biscotti

GENERAL EDITOR
CHUCK WILLIAMS

RECIPES
KRISTINE KIDD

PHOTOGRAPHY
ALLAN ROSENBERG

TIME
LIFE
BOOKS

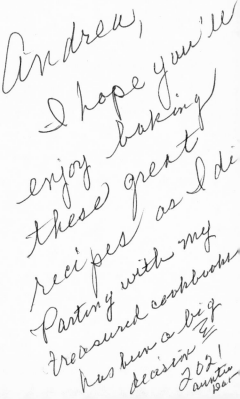

Andrew,
I hope you'll
enjoy baking
these great
recipes as I di
Parting with my
treasured cookbook
has been a big
decision
2021
auntie

TIME-LIFE BOOKS

Time-Life Books is a division of Time Life Inc.
Time-Life is a trademark of Time Warner Inc. U.S.A.

Time-Life Custom Publishing
Vice President and Publisher: Terry Newell
Managing Editor: Donia Ann Steele
Director of Acquisitions: Jennifer L. Pearce
Vice President of Sales and Marketing: Neil Levin
Director of Financial Operations: J. Brian Birky

WILLIAMS-SONOMA
Founder and Vice Chairman: Chuck Williams
Book Buyer: Victoria Kalish

WELDON OWEN INC.
President: John Owen
Vice President and Publisher: Wendely Harvey
Chief Operating Officer: Larry Partington
Associate Publisher: Laurie Wertz
Consulting Editor: Norman Kolpas
Copy Editor: Sharon Silva
Design/Editorial Assistant: Janique Poncelet
Design: John Bull, The Book Design Company
Production: Stephanie Sherman, James Obata,
    Mick Bagnato
Production Coordinator: Tarji Mickelson
Vice President International Sales: Stuart Laurence
Co-Editions Director: Derek Barton
Food Photographer: Allan Rosenberg
Additional Food Photography: Allen V. Lott
Primary Food & Prop Stylist: Sandra Griswold
Food Stylist: Heidi Gintner
Assistant Food Stylist: Danielle Di Salvo
Glossary Illustrations: Alice Harth

The Williams-Sonoma Kitchen Library
conceived and produced by Weldon Owen Inc.
814 Montgomery St., San Francisco, CA 94133

In collaboration with Williams-Sonoma
3250 Van Ness Ave., San Francisco, CA 94109

Printed in China by Toppan Printing Co., LTD.

A Note on Weights and Measures:
All recipes include customary U.S. and metric
measurements. Metric conversions are based on
a standard developed for these books and have
been rounded off. Actual weights may vary.

A Weldon Owen Production

Copyright © 1993 Weldon Owen Inc.
Reprinted in 1993; 1994; 1994; 1994; 1995; 1996; 1997;
    1998

Library of Congress
Cataloging-in-Publication Data:

Kidd, Kristine.
    Cookies & biscotti / general editor,
  Chuck Williams ; recipes, Kristine Kidd ;
  photography, Allan Rosenberg.
        p.   cm. — (Williams-Sonoma kitchen library)
    Includes index.
    ISBN 0-7835-0266-4 (trade) ;
    ISBN 0-7835-0267-2 (lib. bdg.)
    1. Cookies.   2. Cookery, Italian
  I. Williams, Chuck.   II. Title.
    III. Title: Cookies and biscotti.   IV. Series.
TX772.K53   1994
641.8'654—dc20   93-28230
                                             CIP

Contents

CRISP & CRUMBLY COOKIES 15

BAR COOKIES 39

DROP COOKIES 63

SPECIALTY COOKIES 77

Dorothy Lopez

INTRODUCTION

With apologies to apple lovers everywhere, I've always believed that a cookie a day will keep the doctor away.

Cookies are among the most comforting foods imaginable: crisp, soft or chewy; small or large; subtly flavored or sweet as candy; shaped and decorated in a wide array of tempting forms. Faced daily with such an abundant choice of cookies, who couldn't help but feel cheered, feel just a little bit better?

And making cookies doubles the pleasure. Few things you can cook offer as much simple enjoyment. Cookies are easy and fun to make and are an ideal kitchen project in which to enlist the help of children. The happy results are perfect for sharing with family and friends: Attractively wrapped in an airtight tin to keep them fresh, no gift of food is better received!

In that same spirit of sharing, this book offers a generous guide to the world of cookie making. The introductory pages provide all the basics, with an illustrated guide to kitchen equipment and comprehensive step-by-step instructions for mixing, shaping and baking cookies of all kinds. The recipes that follow, each accompanied by a full-color photograph, are organized to help you select just the sort you want to make. There are chapters on crisp and crumbly cookies; bar cookies; drop cookies; and specialty cookies produced by a wide variety of methods. Included, too, are a number of recipes for the highly popular Italian crunchy cookies commonly known as biscotti.

None of these recipes is complicated. All of them are made with readily available ingredients. If you're watching your diet, you can even prepare many of these cookies with margarine or vegetable shortening in place of butter. Simplicity is the key.

So head for the kitchen right now, and start making cookies—for family, friends and, of course, yourself!

Chuck Williams

EQUIPMENT

*Basic and specialized tools for mixing, shaping, baking,
decorating and storing a wide assortment of cookies*

You can easily mix and bake a batch of cookies with
just a small fraction of the equipment shown here. All
you need are measuring cups, bowls and spoons for
mixing the dough; spoons, knives or simply your hands
for shaping it; and a baking sheet and wire rack for
baking and cooling the cookies.

But additional tools make the work even easier, while
expanding your cookie repertoire. A flour sifter, for
example, ensures smoother blending for delicate
mixtures. Electric mixers cut the preparation time of
doughs and batters. A simple cookie press yields fancily
shaped, professional-looking cookies. Assorted airtight
tins keep the baked treats in peak condition.

One more piece of equipment, too big to show here,
merits mention: your oven. Be sure to calibrate it using
a good-quality oven thermometer, to ensure the best
results when following the recipes in this book.

1. Food Processor
Quickly blends cookie doughs
and icings. Choose a model
with a powerful motor; it is
less likely to stall when mixing
stiff doughs.

2. Hand Mixer
Hand-held electric mixer
quickly whisks egg whites and
whips cream.

3. Liquid Measuring Cup
For accurate measuring of
liquid ingredients. Choose
heavy-duty heat-resistant glass,
marked on one side in cups
and ounces, on the other in
milliliters.

4. Wooden Spoons
Traditional tools for mixing
cookie doughs and batters.

5. Mixing Bowls
For easier mixing, choose high-
sided, deep bowls in a range
of sizes. Lips and handles
facilitate pouring.

6. Double Boiler
Ideal for melting chocolate
without scorching. Water
simmers in the lower pan while
ingredients in the upper,
smaller pan are warmed by
steam heat without direct
contact with the water.

7. Dry Measuring Cups
In graduated sizes, for accurate
measuring of dry ingredients.
Straight rims allow ingredients
to be leveled for accuracy.
Choose stainless steel for
accuracy and sturdiness.

8. Zester
Small, sharp-edged holes at
end of stainless-steel blade cut
citrus zest into fine shreds.
Choose a model with a sturdy,
well-attached handle.

9. Kitchen Knives
Paring knife for general cutting
needs; slicing knife for cutting
rolls of refrigerator cookie
dough; serrated bread knife for
slicing biscotti loaves before

11. Wire Whisks
Large flat whisk for stirring batters and beating pastry cream; small balloon whisk for whisking egg whites and whipping cream. Choose sturdy, stainless-steel whisks.

12. Sifter
Turning the handle passes flour through the sifter's fine-mesh screen, giving it a uniform consistency for even blending. May also be used for sifting together several dry ingredients.

13. Electric Mixer
Heavy-duty countertop mixer with stainless-steel bowl assists in mixing stiff cookie doughs or large quantities of any dough or batter.

14. Rolling Pin
The most commonly used rolling pin for cookie doughs. Choose one with ball-bearing handles for smooth rolling, and a hardwood surface. To prevent warping, do not wash; wipe clean with a dry cloth.

15. Tins
Assorted airtight containers with tight-fitting lids keep cookies in peak condition for home storage or gift giving.

16. Spatulas
Small, narrow-bladed spatula neatly spreads icings or other cookie toppings, as well as accurately levels the surface of dry ingredients with the rims of measuring cups. Wider, square-cornered spatula efficiently removes cookies from baking sheets and pans.

17. Measuring Spoons
In graduated sizes, for measuring small quantities of ingredients such as baking powder and salt. Select good-quality, calibrated metal spoons with deep bowls.

18. Baking Pan
For baking brownies and bar cookies. Quality, sturdy aluminum pan conducts heat well.

19. Wire Racks
Rack with small, square grid securely holds small or delicate cookies while they cool. Larger rack with parallel wires supports baking pans or holds larger cookies during cooling.

20. Baking Sheets
Rimless baking sheets make removing cookies with a spatula easier; single raised edge provides the baker with a convenient grip. Dark, heavy-duty metal sheets conduct heat well for faster, more even browning; the new, shiny insulated sheets prevent thin or delicate cookies from browning too quickly.

21. Cookie Cutters
Sturdy tinned or stainless-steel cutters provide a wide variety of shapes.

22. Cookie Press
Packed into the cylinder of the easily assembled tool, cookie dough is pressed out through a variety of design plates to form attractive, uniform shapes.

23. Parchment Paper
Stick-resistant, ovenproof paper for lining baking sheets. The paper facilitates easy removal of cookies to racks to cool and allows for preparing multiple sheets of cookies at a time.

their final baking. Select good-quality, stain-resistant steel blades with firmly anchored, comfortable handles.

10. Kitchen Spoons
A pair of sturdy, stainless-steel spoons for scooping and shaping drop cookie doughs.

CRISP & CRUMBLY COOKIES

As the recipes on pages 15–38 demonstrate, a variety of ingredients and mixing, shaping and baking techniques are used to make crisp and crumbly cookies. Among the simplest are old-fashioned slice-and-bake refrigerator cookies. Shortbread cookie doughs, which have a high proportion of butter to flour, are rolled out and then cut into plain or fanciful shapes with cookie cutters. And Italian biscotti, the crispest of all, are baked first in a cakelike log, and then again in individual slices—hence their name, literally, "twice-cooked."

USING A COOKIE CUTTER

After rolling out the dough, dip the edge of a cookie cutter in flour and press down firmly to cut out the dough. Experiment with assorted shapes and sizes of cutters to create window effects, such as in the strawberry shortcakes shown here (recipe on page 35).

ROLLING DOUGH FOR REFRIGERATOR COOKIES

For slice-and-bake cookies, mix a fairly firm dough and spoon it down the center of a sheet of waxed paper. Roll up inside the paper, forming a log of whatever shape you desire—round, square, rectangular. Refrigerate until firm; then unwrap, slice and bake.

BISCOTTI BASICS

1. Sifting dry ingredients. For a smooth, uniform dough, first sift together the dry ingredients—here, flour, baking soda, baking powder and salt—into a bowl. In a separate bowl combine the moist ingredients. Add the dry mixture to the moist, mixing until a dough forms.

2. Preparing baking sheets. Baking sheets for biscotti are prepared in one of several ways, depending upon the recipe: ungreased, buttered, lined with parchment paper or waxed paper, or, as shown here, lightly buttered and then evenly sprinkled with flour.

3. Shaping logs of dough. Using a large kitchen spoon, spoon the batter onto the prepared baking sheets to form rough log shapes. Flour the palms of your hands and use them to smooth the logs' surfaces. Or, for firmer doughs, shape with your hands on a floured work surface and transfer to sheets.

4. Slicing the baked log. Bake the log until lightly browned and firm to the touch. Remove from the oven, let cool slightly, then, using a serrated knife, cut into slices. Arrange the slices on the baking sheet and finish baking until crisp and golden.

DROP COOKIES

Drop cookies are probably the easiest cookies to prepare (recipes, pages 63–76): Just mix the batter in a bowl, scoop up by the spoonful, drop onto a baking sheet and then slip into the oven. Soft, buttery batters yield cookies that are generally tender and chewy; a longer baking time will usually produce more crisp results.

1. Mixing the batter.
Following the recipe instructions, use an electric mixer or wooden spoon to beat together the softened butter and sugar until light and fluffy. Beat in the eggs, and then the sifted dry ingredients.

2. Dropping the batter.
Scoop up the batter with a tablespoon and use a second spoon to push it off onto an ungreased baking sheet, spacing the cookies about 2 inches (5 cm) apart.

BAR COOKIES

Simple-to-make bar cookies (recipes, pages 39–62)—the most familiar of which are brownies—result from soft, rich batters baked in straight-sided pans. As with a cake, use a toothpick or other test to ensure the mixture bakes just until set and remains moist. Once cooled, the sheet of tender cookies is cut into bite-sized pieces. Lining the pan with aluminum foil makes lifting out the finished cookies easy.

1. Lining the baking pan.
Tear a sheet of foil large enough to cover the bottom and sides of the baking pan. Press the foil into the pan, folding any excess over the rim.

2. Testing for doneness.
How to test for doneness depends upon the recipe. The most common tests include: until the center is springy to the touch, until browned, or, as shown here, until a tester such as a toothpick inserted in the center comes out with a few moist crumbs.

Lemon-Coconut Squares

3. Removing from the pan.
Place the baking pan on a wire rack and let cool to room temperature. To unmold, firmly grasp the foil at opposite ends and lift. Peel back the foil, then cut the cookies into squares or bars.

SPECIALTY COOKIES

Many cookies, classic and contemporary alike (recipes, pages 77–103), take their form from means less conventional than dropping batter, slicing dough or cutting bars. Unique shapes often result from simple hands-on creativity: twisting strips of puff pastry, pressing thumbprints into balls of soft dough, or forming ropes to bake as crescents. An easily assembled cookie press (right) can introduce even more imaginative forms.

Twisting pastry strips.
For crisp cookie sticks such as the cinnamon-poppy sugar twists on page 102, roll out a sheet of puff pastry, brush with beaten egg and sprinkle with sweet seasonings. Cut into strips and twist each strip before placing on a baking sheet.

Pressing thumbprints.
Prepare a slightly soft cookie dough and form into balls, rolling each between your palms to smooth its shape before placing on a baking sheet. Using your thumb, press a well in the center of each ball to hold a filling such as sugar or jam.

Shaping crescents.
For crescent-shaped cookies such as the walnut-cardamom Viennese crescents on page 81, first prepare a pliable dough. Roll a small amount of the dough between your palms to form a rope that tapers at the ends. Place on a baking sheet in a curved crescent shape.

USING A COOKIE PRESS

1. Filling the press.
Prepare a fairly firm but still pliable cookie dough. For easier packing, roll the dough into a log (see page 8) slightly smaller than the diameter and about the same length of the cookie press cylinder. With the top and handle in place, unwrap the dough and slip it into the tube.

2. Choosing a design plate.
Select a design plate from among the choices available. Fit the plate into its holder and screw securely onto the press.

3. Pressing out the dough.
Hold the press upright, securely grasp the handle and, applying even pressure, press out the dough to form cookies. Be sure to read the manufacturer's instructions carefully, as models vary.

TOPPINGS FOR COOKIES

The simple topping recipes on the following pages add even more creativity to the cookie-making process. Cinnamon sugar and vanilla sugar contribute sweet, subtle flavor and a glistening surface when sprinkled over cookies just before they enter the oven. Easy-to-make glazes, coatings and icings (pages 12–13) are used for sandwich cookies and—with the aid of a pastry bag or a common table fork—to create a wide array of artfully decorated confections.

Cinnamon Sugar

This simple preparation, which keeps for months in a covered container at room temperature, is used to add spice to several cookies in this collection. To make terrific cinnamon toast, simply toast one side of a slice of your favorite bread under the broiler (griller), then turn it over, spread the untoasted side with butter and sprinkle with cinnamon sugar. Broil (grill) until the top begins to brown.

½ cup (4 oz/125 g) granulated sugar
1½ teaspoons ground cinnamon

Stir together the sugar and cinnamon in a small bowl. Store in an airtight container.

Makes about ½ cup (4 oz/125 g)

Vanilla Sugar

A quick preparation that captures the incomparable flavor of vanilla bean. It keeps for months in an airtight container and can be substituted for vanilla extract (essence) and sugar in almost any recipe. It is delicious when used in simply flavored sweets that allow the vanilla flavor to come through, or sprinkled over cookies just before baking.

1½ vanilla beans
2 cups (1 lb/500 g) granulated sugar

Cut the vanilla beans into 1½-inch (4-cm) lengths. Place in a food processor fitted with the metal blade or in a blender and process. Add ½ cup (4 oz/125 g) of the sugar and process until the vanilla beans are finely chopped. Add the remaining 1½ cups (12 oz/375 g) sugar and process until thoroughly incorporated.

Strain the sugar through a fine-mesh sieve to remove any large pieces of vanilla bean. Store in an airtight container.

*Makes about 2 cups
(1 lb/500 g)*

Vanilla Cookie-Press Ribbons

Caramel Glaze

Ordinary cookies become something special when drizzled with this easy-to-make glaze. Caramel glaze is normally made by the exacting technique of cooking sugar in a heavy pan until it caramelizes; in this recipe caramel candies are simply melted in a bit of water. Be sure to use good-quality caramels.

8 oz (250 g) caramel candies (about 1 cup packed)
¼ cup (2 fl oz/60 ml) water

Combine the caramels and water in a small, heavy saucepan over low heat. Stir until the caramels melt and the mixture is smooth. Remove from the heat.

The glaze can be applied to cookies in one of two ways: Using a fork or spoon, slowly drizzle the hot glaze over the cookies. Alternatively, spread the glaze atop the cookies using a small icing spatula or a table knife. Let stand until cool, about 30 minutes.

*Makes about ¾ cup
(6 fl oz/180 ml)*

Chocolate Coating

A versatile performer. This scrumptious coating can be spread or drizzled onto cookies, used as a dip for cookies, or become the filling in a sandwich cookie. Be sure to store chocolate-coated cookies in the refrigerator to prevent the chocolate from softening.

8 oz (250 g) semisweet or bittersweet chocolate, chopped
2 teaspoons vegetable shortening

Combine the chocolate and shortening in the top pan of a double boiler. Melt over (not touching) simmering water just until smooth, stirring occasionally. Remove from the heat. Alternatively, melt the chocolate and shortening in a heatproof bowl placed over (not touching) simmering water.

To coat cookie tops with chocolate, dip the tops in the hot chocolate or, using a small icing spatula or a table knife, spread the chocolate over the tops. Set the cookies, chocolate sides up, on a baking sheet.

To coat cookies decoratively, dip one end of each cookie in the chocolate. Set on aluminum foil–lined baking sheets.

To drizzle the chocolate decoratively over cookies, dip the tines of a fork in the chocolate and wave back and forth over the cookies.

To create a cookie sandwich, spread the chocolate over the flat side of one cookie. Top with a second cookie, flat side down.

Refrigerate all chocolate-coated cookies until the chocolate sets.

Makes about ¾ cup (6 fl oz/180 ml)

*Chocolate Chip-
Pecan Cookies*

CHOCOLATE TOPPINGS FOR COOKIES

Melting the chocolate.
Use a double boiler, or place a heatproof bowl inside the rim of a saucepan. Fill the bottom pan with enough water to come close to the top pan or bowl without touching it. Bring the water to a low simmer, add the chocolate and stir gently until melted.

Dipping by hand.
To coat one side of large cookies such as biscotti, grasp a cookie with your fingers and dip carefully into the warm chocolate.

Drizzling with chocolate.
For a simple decoration, use a spoon or fork to drizzle melted chocolate over the tops of cookies.

Confectioners' Sugar Icing

A basic icing that gives a finished look to baked treats whether used in its natural off-white state or altered with food coloring. Spread it on cookies or, for a more elegant look, use a pastry bag to pipe on decorative patterns. Or take your decorating one step further by sprinkling the freshly iced cookies with colored crystal sugars or other sprinkles.

3 cups (12 oz/375 g) confectioners' (icing) sugar
2 tablespoons milk, or as needed
1½ tablespoons fresh lemon juice
food coloring, optional
colored crystal sugars, optional

Place the confectioners' sugar in a bowl. Add 2 tablespoons milk and the lemon juice and stir until smooth. If the mixture is too thick to pipe or spread, add a small amount of milk.

To color the icing, mix in food coloring, adding it by drops until the desired shade is achieved. Alternatively, divide the icing among several bowls and tint each portion a different color.

To spread the icing over cookies, use a small icing spatula or a table knife.

To pipe the icing atop cookies, spoon the icing into a pastry bag fitted with a small plain tip. Pipe decoratively over the cookies.

To drizzle the icing decoratively over cookies, dip the tines of a fork in the icing and wave back and forth over the cookies.

To decorate the icing-topped cookies with colored sugars, sprinkle on the sugars as soon as the cookies are iced.

Place the cookies on a flat surface until the icing sets, about 2 hours.

Makes about 1 cup (8 fl oz/250 ml)

Almond, Lemon and Anise Biscotti

2 eggs
¾ cup (6 oz/185 g) granulated sugar
½ cup (4 fl oz/125 ml) vegetable oil
1 tablespoon grated lemon zest
2 teaspoons aniseeds, crushed
1¼ teaspoons baking powder
1 teaspoon vanilla extract (essence)
¼ teaspoon salt
2 cups (10 oz/315 g) all-purpose (plain) flour
1 cup (5½ oz/170 g) whole almonds, coarsely chopped
plain granulated sugar or vanilla sugar
  (recipe on page 11)

A new twist on a traditional recipe for mandelbrot, *the Jewish version of biscotti. Anise adds an exotic flavor; without it, the recipe turns out delicious lemon cookies.*

♡

*P*reheat an oven to 350°F (180°C).

In a large bowl combine the eggs, the ¾ cup (6 oz/185 g) sugar, oil, lemon zest, aniseeds, baking powder, vanilla and salt. Whisk to blend. Add the flour and almonds and stir until a dough forms. Turn out onto a floured surface and knead until smooth, about 10 turns. Divide the dough in half.

Form each half into a log 2 inches (5 cm) in diameter. Carefully transfer the logs to an ungreased baking sheet, spacing them well apart. Sprinkle the tops with additional sugar or vanilla sugar.

Bake until firm to the touch, about 30 minutes (logs will spread during baking). Remove from the oven and let cool for 10 minutes. Leave the oven set at 350°F (180°C).

Using a spatula carefully transfer the logs to a work surface. Using a serrated knife cut crosswise into slices ½ inch (12 mm) thick. Arrange the slices cut-side down on the baking sheet. Return to the oven and bake until brown, about 20 minutes.

Transfer the cookies to wire racks to cool. Store in an airtight container at room temperature for up to 2 weeks.

Makes about 3 dozen

Christmas Spice Cutouts

½ cup (2 oz/60 g) walnuts

2 cups (10 oz/315 g) all-purpose (plain) flour

¾ cup (6 oz/185 g) firmly packed golden brown sugar

½ teaspoon ground cloves

½ teaspoon ground ginger

½ teaspoon ground allspice

½ teaspoon ground cinnamon

½ teaspoon baking soda (bicarbonate of soda)

½ cup (¼ lb/125 g) unsalted butter, at room temperature

2 teaspoons vanilla extract (essence)

¼ cup (3 oz/90 g) honey

1 egg

colored crystal sugars

A recipe guaranteed to give your house the aroma of the holidays. If you like, omit the colored crystal sugars and spread the cookies with confectioners' sugar icing (page 13) after baking and cooling.

♡

*I*n a food processor fitted with the metal blade or in a blender, finely grind the walnuts (do not grind to a paste). Add ¼ cup (1½ oz/45 g) of the flour and ¼ cup (2 oz/60 g) of the brown sugar and grind to a powder; set aside. Sift together the remaining flour, the spices and baking soda into a bowl; set aside. Combine the butter, vanilla and the remaining brown sugar in a large bowl. Using an electric mixer set on high speed, beat until light and fluffy. Beat in the honey and egg. Reduce the speed to low, add the flour-spice mixture and the nut mixture and mix just until incorporated. Gather the dough into a ball, then divide in half. Form each half into a flat disk. Wrap the disks in separate sheets of waxed paper and chill until firm, at least 1 hour or as long as overnight.

Preheat an oven to 350°F (180°C). Generously butter baking sheets. Flour 1 disk and place between 2 sheets of waxed paper. Roll out the dough ¼ inch (6 mm) thick. Using decoratively shaped cutters, cut out cookies. Transfer to the prepared sheets, spacing them ½ inch (12 mm) apart. Sprinkle with colored crystal sugars. Gather up the scraps into a flat disk and chill.

Bake the cookies until lightly golden, about 10 minutes. Transfer the cookies to wire racks to cool. Repeat with the remaining dough portion. Finally, roll out the scraps and cut and bake in the same manner.

Store refrigerated in an airtight container for up to 2 weeks.

Makes about 3 dozen

Walnut, Chocolate and Ginger Shortbread Fans

1 cup (5 oz/155 g) all-purpose (plain) flour
2 tablespoons plus 2 teaspoons cornstarch (cornflour)
¼ teaspoon salt
½ cup (¼ lb/125 g) unsalted butter, at room temperature
⅓ cup (3 oz/90 g) granulated sugar
¾ teaspoon vanilla extract (essence)
½ cup (2 oz/60 g) walnuts, finely chopped
⅓ cup (2 oz/60 g) miniature semisweet chocolate chips
3 tablespoons firmly packed chopped crystallized ginger
vanilla sugar, optional (recipe on page 11)

The perfect accompaniment to fresh berries for a delightful dinner party dessert. It is easy to make the pretty shape: Press the dough into a pie dish, then cut it into wedges. If you use a metal pie pan, you may have to increase the baking time.

♡

*P*reheat an oven to 350°F (180°C). Butter a 10-inch (25-cm) glass pie dish.

In a bowl stir together the flour, cornstarch and salt; set aside.

Combine the butter, granulated sugar and vanilla in a large bowl. Using an electric mixer set on high speed, beat until light and fluffy. Reduce the speed to low, add the flour mixture and mix until beginning to gather together. Then mix in the walnuts, chocolate chips and ginger.

Press the dough into the bottom of the prepared dish, building up the edges so they reach ½ inch (12 mm) up the sides. Using a fork crimp the edges. Using a sharp knife and a ruler as a guide, cut into 12 wedges. Be sure to cut all the way through the dough. Pierce each wedge 3 times with a fork. Sprinkle with vanilla sugar, if desired.

Bake until barely firm to the touch and brown on the edges, about 30 minutes. Transfer the pie dish to a wire rack and recut the wedges. Let the cookies cool. Gently remove from the dish with a knife. Store in an airtight container at room temperature for up to 1 week.

Makes 1 dozen

Chocolate Chip Biscotti

2 cups (10 oz/315 g) all-purpose (plain) flour

1½ teaspoons baking powder

1 teaspoon ground cinnamon

⅛ teaspoon salt

½ cup (¼ lb/125 g) unsalted butter, at room temperature

½ cup (3½ oz/105 g) firmly packed golden brown sugar

½ cup (4 oz/125 g) granulated sugar

1 tablespoon instant espresso powder

2 eggs

1 cup (4 oz/125 g) coarsely chopped walnuts

1 cup (6 oz/185 g) semisweet chocolate chips

Delicious as is, these cookies are even better when dipped in chocolate coating or drizzled with caramel glaze (recipes on page 12). Sprinkling cinnamon sugar (page 11) over the unbaked dough loaves is another tasty option.

♡

*P*reheat an oven to 325°F (165°C). Butter 2 baking sheets.

Sift together the flour, baking powder, cinnamon and salt into a bowl; set aside.

Combine the butter, brown sugar, granulated sugar and espresso powder in a large bowl. Using an electric mixer set on high speed, beat until light and fluffy. Mix in the eggs, one at a time, and beat until light and fluffy, about 2 minutes. Reduce the speed to low, add the walnuts and chocolate chips and mix in. Add the flour mixture and mix just until incorporated.

Divide the dough in half. Place each half on a prepared baking sheet. Using lightly floured hands, form each half into a log 3 inches (7.5 cm) wide and ¾ inch (2 cm) high.

Bake until firm to the touch, about 25 minutes (logs will spread during baking). Remove from the oven and let cool for 5 minutes. Leave the oven set at 325°F (165°C).

Using a spatula carefully transfer the logs to a work surface. Using a serrated knife cut on the diagonal into slices ½ inch (12 mm) thick. Arrange the slices cut-side down on the baking sheets and bake until the bottoms are brown, about 10 minutes. Remove from the oven and turn the slices over. Bake until the bottoms are brown, about 10 minutes longer. Transfer the cookies to wire racks to cool. Store in an airtight container at room temperature for up to 2 weeks.

Makes about 3 dozen

Cinnamon–Chocolate Chip Refrigerator Cookies

¾ cup (6 oz/185 g) unsalted butter, at
   room temperature
½ cup (4 oz/125 g) granulated sugar
1½ teaspoons grated orange zest
1¼ teaspoons ground cinnamon
¼ teaspoon salt
2 egg yolks
1¾ cups (9 oz/280 g) all-purpose
   (plain) flour
1 cup (6 oz/185 g) miniature semisweet
   chocolate chips
cinnamon sugar (recipe on page 11)

A delicious variation on the traditional Mexican wedding cookie, flavored with cinnamon, chocolate and orange zest. The ideal partner for cups of steaming hot chocolate.

♡

Combine the butter, granulated sugar, orange zest, cinnamon and salt in a large bowl. Using an electric mixer set on high speed, beat until light and fluffy. Add the egg yolks and beat until light and fluffy. Reduce the speed to low, add the flour and chocolate chips and mix just until incorporated.

Turn the dough out onto a lightly floured work surface. Divide in half. Roll each piece between your palms and the work surface to form a log 1½ inches (4 cm) in diameter. Wrap the logs tightly in plastic wrap and refrigerate until firm, about 1 hour or as long as overnight.

Preheat an oven to 350°F (180°C). Lightly butter baking sheets. Unwrap the dough and cut each log into rounds ¼ inch (6 mm) thick. Transfer to the prepared baking sheets, spacing 1½ inches (4 cm) apart.

Bake until the edges are brown, about 15 minutes. Transfer the cookies to wire racks and let cool for 5 minutes.

Put the cinnamon sugar in a bowl. Add several warm cookies and toss to coat with the sugar. Return the cookies to the racks to cool completely. Repeat with the remaining cookies. Store in an airtight container at room temperature for up to 5 days.

Makes about 4 dozen

Pecan-Lemon Shortbread Hearts

1½ cups (7½ oz/235 g) all-purpose (plain) flour
½ cup (4 oz/125 g) granulated sugar
¼ cup (1 oz/30 g) cornstarch (cornflour)
1 tablespoon plus 1 teaspoon grated lemon zest
¼ teaspoon salt
¾ cup (6 oz/185 g) unsalted butter, chilled, cut into ½-inch (12-mm) pieces
½ teaspoon vanilla extract (essence)
1 cup (4 oz/125 g) pecans
vanilla sugar, optional (recipe on page 11)

These pretty, delicate cookies are perfect with coffee or as the finish to a romantic meal. Cut them into any shape you like and sprinkle with vanilla sugar to liven them up. It is fun to use several sizes of cutters, too.

♡

Preheat an oven to 350°F (180°C).

In a food processor fitted with the metal blade, combine the flour, granulated sugar, cornstarch, lemon zest and salt. Process briefly until well mixed. Add the butter and vanilla and, using rapid off-on pulses, cut in until the mixture resembles a fine meal. Add the pecans and process until finely chopped.

Transfer the mixture to a large sheet of waxed paper and gather together into a flat disk. Top with a second sheet of waxed paper. Roll out the dough ¼ inch (6 mm) thick. Using a 3-inch (7.5-cm) or 1½-inch (4-cm) heart-shaped cutter, cut out cookies. Transfer to ungreased baking sheets, spacing them ½ inch (12 mm) apart. Gather up the scraps, roll out again and cut out additional cookies. Sprinkle the cookies with vanilla sugar, if desired.

Bake until just beginning to color, about 20 minutes. Transfer the baking sheets to wire racks and let cool for 5 minutes. Transfer the cookies to the racks to cool completely. Store in an airtight container at room temperature for up to 1 week.

Makes about 2 dozen 3-inch (7.5-cm) cookies

Chocolate-Hazelnut Biscotti

♡

4 oz (125 g) semisweet chocolate, coarsely chopped

1 cup (7 oz/220 g) firmly packed light brown sugar

1¾ cups (9 oz/280 g) unbleached all-purpose (plain) flour

⅓ cup (1 oz/30 g) unsweetened cocoa, preferably Dutch process

1½ tablespoons instant espresso powder

1 teaspoon baking soda (bicarbonate of soda)

¼ teaspoon salt

3 eggs

1¼ teaspoons vanilla extract (essence)

½ teaspoon almond extract (essence)

1 cup (5 oz/155 g) hazelnuts (filberts), toasted and coarsely chopped

chocolate coating (recipe on page 12)

Preheat an oven to 300°F (150°C). Line a large baking sheet with parchment paper or waxed paper.

In a food processor fitted with the metal blade, combine the chocolate and brown sugar and process until the chocolate is very fine; set aside. Alternatively, use a blender, processing 1 oz (30 g) chocolate and ¼ cup (2 oz/60 g) sugar at a time.

Sift together the flour, cocoa, espresso powder, baking soda and salt into a bowl; set aside. Combine the eggs, vanilla extract and almond extract in a large bowl. Using an electric mixer set on medium speed, beat to blend. On low speed mix in the sugar and flour mixtures until a stiff dough forms, adding the hazelnuts when about half mixed.

On a floured surface divide the dough in half. Form each half into a log 12 inches (30 cm) long. Transfer the logs to the prepared baking sheet, spacing them well apart, and pat to even the shapes. Bake until almost firm to the touch, about 50 minutes (logs will spread during baking). Remove from the oven and let cool for 10 minutes. Leave the oven set at 300°F (150°C).

Using a spatula carefully transfer the logs to a work surface. Using a serrated knife cut on the diagonal into slices ½–¾ inch (12 mm–2 cm) thick. Arrange the slices cut-side down on the baking sheet. Bake 25 minutes. Turn the slices over and bake until crisp and dry, about 25 minutes longer. Turn off the oven and let cool completely in oven with the door slightly ajar.

Dip one side of the cooled cookies in the hot chocolate coating and set chocolate-side up on a baking sheet. Refrigerate until set. Store refrigerated in an airtight container for up to 2 weeks.

Makes about 2½ dozen

Vanilla Bean Refrigerator Cookies

1¾ cups (7 oz/220 g) all-purpose (plain) flour, sifted before measuring
1½ teaspoons baking powder
⅛ teaspoon salt
½ cup (¼ lb/125 g) unsalted butter, at room temperature
about 1⅓ cups (11 oz/345 g) vanilla sugar *(recipe on page 11)*
1 egg

The vanilla aroma really comes through in these crisp cookies. For cute miniature cookies, form the dough into logs 1 inch (2.5 cm) in diameter.

♡

Sift together the flour, baking powder and salt into a bowl; set aside. Place the butter in a large bowl and, using an electric mixer set on high speed, beat until light and fluffy. Add 1 cup (8 oz/250 g) of the vanilla sugar and beat until thoroughly incorporated. Add the egg and beat until light and fluffy. Reduce the speed to low, add the flour mixture and mix just until incorporated.

Spoon the dough in a rough log 10 inches (25 cm) long down the center of a sheet of waxed paper. Fold 1 side of the paper over the dough and, pressing with your hands, form into an even oblong, square, circle, rectangle or triangle about 10 inches (25 cm) long. Wrap tightly in the waxed paper and refrigerate until firm, at least 4 hours or as long as overnight.

Preheat an oven to 400°F (200°C). Butter baking sheets. Unwrap the dough and transfer to a work surface. Carefully cut into slices ¼ inch (6 mm) thick. Transfer the cookies to the prepared baking sheets, spacing 1 inch (2.5 cm) apart. Sprinkle with the remaining vanilla sugar.

Bake until the edges are brown, about 12 minutes. Transfer the cookies to wire racks to cool. Store in an airtight container for up to 5 days.

Makes about 3½ dozen

Pine Nut and Honey Biscotti

2 cups (10 oz/315 g) all-purpose (plain) flour

1 teaspoon baking powder

½ teaspoon baking soda (bicarbonate of soda)

½ teaspoon salt

½ cup (4 fl oz/125 ml) vegetable oil

½ cup (4 oz/125 g) granulated sugar

½ cup (6 oz/185 g) honey

2 eggs

2 teaspoons grated orange zest

1 teaspoon vanilla extract (essence)

1½ cups (8 oz/250 g) pine nuts, lightly toasted

The characteristic dryness of this tasty cookie makes it a wonderful companion for a cup of espresso or a glass of sweet wine. For a different flavor, substitute almonds for the pine nuts.

♡

Sift together the flour, baking powder, baking soda and salt into a bowl. In a large bowl combine the oil, sugar, honey, eggs, orange zest and vanilla and stir until smooth. Add the flour mixture and stir until smooth. Fold in the pine nuts. Cover and refrigerate until well chilled, about 3 hours.

Preheat an oven to 350°F (180°C). Butter and flour 2 large baking sheets. Spoon two thirds of the batter into 2 rough log shapes on 1 sheet, spacing them well apart, and the remaining batter into 1 log shape on the second sheet. Using well-floured hands, form into smooth logs 2 inches (5 cm) wide and 1 inch (2.5 cm) high.

Bake until just springy to the touch, about 25 minutes (logs will spread during baking). Remove from the oven and let cool slightly on the baking sheets. Leave the oven set at 350°F (180°C).

Using a spatula carefully transfer the logs to a work surface. Using a serrated knife cut crosswise into slices ½ inch (12 mm) thick. Arrange the slices cut-side down on the baking sheets and bake 5 minutes. Remove from the oven and turn the slices over. Bake until brown, about 5 minutes longer. Transfer the cookies to wire racks to cool. Store in an airtight container at room temperature for up to 2 weeks.

Makes about 4 dozen

English Toffee Shortbread

1 cup (5 oz/155 g) all-purpose (plain)
    flour
⅓ cup (2½ oz/75 g) firmly packed
    brown sugar
2½ tablespoons cornstarch (cornflour)
⅛ teaspoon salt
½ cup (¼ lb/125 g) unsalted butter,
    chilled, cut into ½-inch (12-mm)
    pieces
¾ teaspoon vanilla extract (essence)
½ cup (2 oz/60 g) pecans
⅓ cup (2 oz/60 g) finely chopped
    English toffee such as Heath Bar or
    Almond Roca
plain granulated sugar or vanilla sugar
    (recipe on page 11)

Cut these into simple rounds or other decorative shapes, then take them along to a party. They make the perfect hostess gift.

♥

*P*reheat an oven to 350°F (180°C).

   In a food processor fitted with the metal blade, combine the flour, brown sugar, cornstarch and salt. Process briefly until well mixed. Add the butter and vanilla and, using rapid off-on pulses, process until the mixture resembles a fine meal. Add the pecans and process until finely chopped. Add the toffee and process just until mixed in.

   Transfer the mixture to a large sheet of waxed paper. Gather together into a flat disk. Top with a second sheet of waxed paper. Roll out the dough ¼ inch (6 mm) thick. Using a 3-inch (7.5-cm) round or decorative cutter, cut out cookies. Transfer to an ungreased baking sheet. Gather up the scraps, roll out again and cut out additional cookies. Sprinkle the cookies with plain sugar or vanilla sugar.

   Bake until just beginning to color, about 20 minutes. Transfer the baking sheet to a wire rack and let cool for 5 minutes. Transfer the cookies to the rack to cool completely. Store in an airtight container at room temperature for up to 5 days.

Makes about 16

Strawberry Shortcakes

2¼ cups (11½ oz/360 g) all-purpose
  (plain) flour
¼ cup (1 oz/30 g) cornstarch
  (cornflour)
¼ teaspoon salt
¾ cup (6 oz/185 g) unsalted butter, at
  room temperature
1½ teaspoons vanilla extract (essence)
1½ teaspoons grated lemon zest
1 cup (8 oz/250 g) granulated sugar
1 whole egg
1 egg yolk
strawberry jam
confectioners' (icing) sugar, optional

*The classic summer dessert turned into a delicate sandwich cookie.
For an even prettier presentation, use a second, smaller cutter to cut
a window in each cookie top before baking (see page 8).*

♡

Sift together the flour, cornstarch and salt into a bowl; set aside.
Combine the butter, vanilla and lemon zest in a large bowl.
Using an electric mixer set on high speed, beat until light. Add
the granulated sugar and continue to beat until thoroughly
incorporated. Add the whole egg and egg yolk and beat until light
and fluffy. On low speed add the flour mixture and mix just until
incorporated. Gather the dough into a ball, then divide into
thirds. Flatten each third into a flat disk. Wrap the disks in
separate sheets of waxed paper and chill until firm, at least 1 hour
or as long as overnight.

Preheat an oven to 350°F (180°C). Butter baking sheets. Flour
1 disk and place between 2 large sheets of waxed paper. Roll out
the dough ⅛ inch (3 mm) thick. Using 3-inch (7.5-cm)
decoratively shaped cutters, cut out cookies. Transfer to the
prepared sheets, spacing ½ inch (12 mm) apart. Chill for 10
minutes. Gather up the scraps and chill as well.

Bake the cookies until the edges are golden, about 10 minutes.
Transfer the cookies to a wire rack to cool. Repeat with the
remaining 2 dough portions. Finally, roll out the scraps and cut,
chill and bake in the same manner.

Spread jam on the bottoms of half of the cookies, spreading
only lightly at the edges. Top with the remaining cookies, bottom
sides down. Sieve confectioners' sugar over the tops, if desired.
Store refrigerated in an airtight container for up to 1 week.

Makes about 3 dozen sandwich cookies

Pistachio-Orange Biscotti

1¾ cups (9 oz/280 g) all-purpose (plain) flour

½ teaspoon baking soda (bicarbonate of soda)

½ teaspoon baking powder

⅛ teaspoon salt

½ cup (¼ lb/125 g) unsalted butter, at room temperature

1 cup (8 oz/250 g) granulated sugar

2 tablespoons grated orange zest

1½ teaspoons vanilla extract (essence)

2 eggs

1½ cups (6 oz/185 g) unsalted shelled pistachio nuts

A terrific recipe for long-keeping cookies. Try enhancing them with either chocolate coating or caramel glaze (recipes on page 12).

♡

Sift together the flour, baking soda, baking powder and salt into a bowl; set aside. Combine the butter, sugar, orange zest and vanilla in a large bowl. Using an electric mixer set on high speed, beat until light and fluffy. Mix in the eggs, one at a time, beating well after each addition. Reduce the speed to low, add the pistachios and mix in. Add the flour mixture and mix just until incorporated. Cover and refrigerate until well chilled, about 1 hour.

Preheat an oven to 350°F (180°C). Butter and flour a large baking sheet.

Divide the dough in half. Using lightly floured hands, roll each half on a lightly floured surface into a log 1½ inches (4 cm) in diameter. Arrange the logs on the prepared baking sheet, spacing them 5 inches (12 cm) apart.

Bake until light brown and firm to the touch, about 30 minutes (logs will spread during baking). Remove from the oven and let cool slightly on the baking sheet. Leave the oven set at 350°F (180°C).

Using a spatula carefully transfer the logs to a work surface. Using a serrated knife cut on the diagonal into slices ¾ inch (2 cm) thick. Arrange the slices cut-side down on the baking sheet and bake until golden brown, about 15 minutes. Transfer the cookies to wire racks to cool. Store in an airtight container at room temperature for up to 2 weeks.

Makes about 3 dozen

Chocolate Mint Brownies

FOR THE BROWNIES:

4 oz (125 g) unsweetened chocolate,
   chopped

½ cup (¼ lb/125 g) unsalted butter

1¼ cups (10 oz/315 g) granulated sugar

1½ teaspoons peppermint extract
   (essence)

¾ teaspoon vanilla extract (essence)

¼ teaspoon salt

3 eggs

¾ cup (4 oz/125 g) all-purpose (plain)
   flour

FOR THE ICING:

1 cup (4 oz/125 g) confectioners' (icing)
   sugar

3 tablespoons unsalted butter, at room
   temperature

1 tablespoon milk, or as needed

2 teaspoons peppermint extract (essence)

A rich chocolate base is topped with a thin layer of mint icing. For a double treat, serve with mint chocolate-chip ice cream.

❋

Preheat an oven to 325°F (165°C). Line an 8-inch (20-cm) square baking pan with aluminum foil.

To make the brownies, combine the chocolate and butter in a large, heavy saucepan over low heat. Stir until melted and smooth. Let cool slightly.

Whisk the sugar, peppermint extract, vanilla extract and salt into the chocolate mixture. Whisk in the eggs, one at a time, whisking well after each addition, then continue to whisk until the mixture is velvety. Add the flour and whisk just until blended. Pour the batter into the prepared pan.

Bake until the top is just springy to the touch and a toothpick inserted in the center comes out with a few moist crumbs attached, about 40 minutes. Let cool in the pan on a wire rack.

To make the icing, combine the sugar, butter, 1 tablespoon milk and the peppermint extract in a food processor fitted with the metal blade. Process until smooth, thinning with more milk if necessary (the icing should be thick). Or beat with an electric mixer set on high speed.

Using the foil lift the sheet of brownies from the pan and place on a work surface. Peel back the foil sides. Spread the icing over the cooled brownies. Cut into 16 squares. Remove the brownies from the foil. Wrap individually in plastic wrap and store in the refrigerator for up to 3 days.

Makes 16

Linzertorte Bars

1½ cups (6 oz/185 g) walnuts or slivered
   blanched almonds
3 tablespoons plus ½ cup (4 oz/125 g)
   granulated sugar
1 cup (5 oz/155 g) all-purpose (plain)
   flour
½ teaspoon baking powder
½ teaspoon ground cinnamon
⅛ teaspoon ground cloves
⅛ teaspoon salt
¾ cup (6 oz/185 g) unsalted butter, at
   room temperature
¾ teaspoon vanilla extract (essence)
2 egg yolks
1 cup (10 oz/315 g) apricot or raspberry
   preserves
confectioners' (icing) sugar

The classic Viennese pastry transformed into quick-and-easy cookies. Fill them with your favorite preserves—or even marmalade.

✺

*P*reheat an oven to 350°F (180°C). Line a 9-inch (23-cm) square baking pan with aluminum foil. Butter the foil.

In a food processor fitted with the metal blade or in a blender, place the nuts and coarsely chop. Add the 3 table-spoons sugar and process finely. Into a separate bowl sift together the flour, baking powder, cinnamon, cloves and salt. Set both mixtures aside. Combine the butter, the ½ cup (4 oz/125 g) sugar and the vanilla in a large bowl. Using an electric mixer set on high speed, beat until light and fluffy. Add the egg yolks and beat until fluffy. Reduce the speed to low, add the nut and flour mixtures and mix just until blended.

Spread 1¾ cups (14 fl oz/425 ml) of the batter in the prepared pan. Top with the preserves, leaving a ½-inch (12-mm) border. Spoon the remaining batter into a pastry bag fitted with a ¼-inch (6-mm) plain tip. Pipe the batter in a lattice pattern atop the preserves. Refrigerate for 20 minutes.

Bake until the preserves begin to bubble and the crust is just firm to the touch, about 40 minutes. Let cool in the pan on a wire rack.

Using the foil lift the sheet from the pan. Peel back the foil sides. Cut into 20 squares. Sieve confectioners' sugar evenly over the tops. Remove the bars from the foil. Store in an airtight container at room temperature for up to 5 days.

Makes 20

Lemon-Coconut Squares

FOR THE CRUST:

1 cup (5 oz/155 g) all-purpose (plain)
    flour
¼ cup (2 oz/60 g) granulated sugar
¼ teaspoon salt
6 tablespoons (3 oz/90 g) unsalted
    butter, chilled, cut into ½-inch
    (12-mm) pieces
¾ cup (2½ oz/75 g) toasted flaked
    coconut

FOR THE FILLING:

¾ cup (6 oz/185 g) granulated sugar
2 eggs
3 tablespoons fresh lemon juice
1 tablespoon grated lemon zest
½ teaspoon baking powder
pinch of salt

confectioners' (icing) sugar

Coconut adds a special twist in this recipe for a picnic favorite, but feel free to vary the flavor by substituting chopped almonds or hazelnuts (filberts). To make a stripe pattern on the cookies, place strips of parchment paper atop the cooled cookies, then dust with confectioners' (icing) sugar.

❈

Preheat an oven to 350°F (180°C). Line an 8-inch (20-cm) square baking pan with aluminum foil. Butter the foil.

To make the crust, in a food processor fitted with the metal blade combine the flour, sugar and salt. Process briefly until well mixed. Add the butter and coconut and process until the mixture resembles a fine meal. Transfer to the prepared pan and press into the bottom to form a crust. Bake until light brown around the edges, about 35 minutes.

Meanwhile, to make the filling, combine the sugar, eggs, lemon juice and zest, baking powder and salt in a food processor fitted with the metal blade or in a blender. Process until smooth.

When the crust is ready, pour the filling onto the hot crust. Continue to bake until the filling begins to brown around the edges and is just springy to the touch, about 35 minutes longer. Let cool in the pan on a wire rack.

Using the foil lift the sheet from the pan and place on a work surface. Gently peel back the foil sides. Cut into 16 squares. Sieve confectioners' sugar evenly over the tops. Remove the squares from the foil. Store in an airtight container in the refrigerator for up to 5 days.

Makes 16

White Chocolate and Macadamia Nut Blondies

½ cup (¼ lb/125 g) unsalted butter, at room temperature

1¼ cups (9 oz/280 g) firmly packed golden brown sugar

2 teaspoons instant espresso powder

1 teaspoon vanilla extract (essence)

2 eggs

1 cup (5 oz/155 g) all-purpose (plain) flour

¾ cup (4 oz/125 g) macadamia nuts, coarsely chopped

3–4 oz (90–125 g) white chocolate, coarsely chopped

A rich, gooey and delicious treat that travels well on such excursions as picnics and bicycling trips. Drizzle the blondies with caramel glaze (recipe on page 12) if you're feeling indulgent.

✳

Preheat an oven to 350°F (180°C). Butter an 8-inch (20-cm) square baking pan.

Combine the butter, brown sugar, espresso powder and vanilla in a large bowl. Using an electric mixer set on high speed, beat until light and fluffy. Beat in the eggs, one at a time, then beat at high speed until very fluffy, about 2 minutes. Reduce the speed to low, add the flour and mix in. Continuing to mix on low speed, fold in the nuts and white chocolate just until blended. Spread the batter in the prepared pan.

Bake until a toothpick inserted in the center comes out clean, about 40 minutes. Let cool in the pan on a wire rack. Cut into 24 bars. Wrap individually in plastic wrap and store at room temperature for up to 3 days.

Makes 2 dozen

Fig and Walnut Hermits

2 cups (10 oz/315 g) all-purpose (plain) flour

1 teaspoon ground cinnamon

¾ teaspoon baking soda (bicarbonate of soda)

¾ teaspoon baking powder

½ teaspoon salt

½ teaspoon ground allspice

½ cup (¼ lb/125 g) unsalted butter, at room temperature

½ cup (3½ oz/105 g) firmly packed dark brown sugar

2 eggs

½ cup (4 fl oz/125 ml) unsulfured light molasses

1 cup (5 oz/155 g) chopped dried Calimyrna figs

1 cup (4 oz/125 g) coarsely chopped walnuts

½ recipe confectioners' sugar icing (recipe on page 13)

Filled with fruit and nuts and glazed with confectioners' sugar icing, these molasses bars make fabulous lunchbox or picnic treats.

✳

Preheat an oven to 350°F (180°C). Butter a 9-by-13-inch (23-by-33-cm) baking dish.

Sift together the flour, cinnamon, baking soda, baking powder, salt and allspice into a bowl; set aside. Combine the butter and brown sugar in a large bowl. Using an electric mixer set on high speed, beat until fluffy. Beat in the eggs, one at a time, then continue beating until very fluffy, about 2 minutes. Mix in the molasses; do not worry if the mixture appears curdled. Reduce the speed to low, add the flour mixture and mix just until blended. Fold in the figs and walnuts. Spread the batter in the prepared dish.

Bake until the top is just springy to the touch, about 30 minutes. Let cool in the dish on a wire rack. Spread the icing evenly over the top and let stand until set, about 2 hours.

Cut into bars 3 inches (7.5 cm) by 1½ inches (4 cm). Wrap individually in plastic wrap and store at room temperature for up to 3 days.

Makes about 2 dozen

Hazelnut-Orange Brownies

3 oz (90 g) unsweetened chocolate,
  chopped
6 tablespoons (3 oz/90 g) unsalted butter
2 eggs
1 cup (8 oz/250 g) granulated sugar
1 tablespoon grated orange zest
¾ teaspoon vanilla extract (essence)
pinch of salt
¼ cup (1½ oz/45 g) all-purpose (plain)
  flour
¾ cup (4 oz/125 g) hazelnuts (filberts),
  toasted, skinned and coarsely chopped

Simple and sophisticated, these unusual treats will stay fresh for up to 3 days when wrapped individually in plastic wrap. They make a terrific hostess gift.

❋

Preheat an oven to 350°F (180°C). Butter and flour an 8-inch (20-cm) square baking dish.

Combine the chocolate and butter in a heavy saucepan over low heat and stir until melted and smooth. Set aside.

Place the eggs in a large bowl and whisk until foamy. Whisk in the sugar, orange zest, vanilla and salt until thoroughly incorporated. Stir in the chocolate mixture. Add the flour and mix just until blended. Fold in the hazelnuts. Spread the batter in the prepared dish.

Bake until the top is just springy to the touch and a toothpick inserted in the center comes out with a few moist crumbs attached, about 30 minutes. Let cool in the pan on a wire rack. Cut into 9 squares. Wrap individually in plastic wrap and store at room temperature for up to 3 days.

Makes 9

Caramel-Macadamia Bars

FOR THE PASTRY:

½ cup (2½ oz/75 g) all-purpose (plain) flour

¼ cup (1 oz/30 g) cornstarch (cornflour)

¼ teaspoon salt

¾ cup (6 oz/185 g) unsalted butter, at room temperature

⅓ cup (3 oz/90 g) granulated sugar

1¼ teaspoons grated lemon zest

FOR THE TOPPING:

6 tablespoons (3 oz/90 g) unsalted butter

¼ cup (2 oz/60 g) plus 2 tablespoons firmly packed dark brown sugar

¼ cup (3 oz/90 g) honey

1¾ cups (9 oz/280 g) salted macadamia nuts

1½ tablespoons heavy (double) cream

Serve these chewy sweets as part of a dessert buffet. The macadamia nuts can be replaced with pine nuts, cashews, pecans or a mixture.

❋

Preheat an oven to 350°F (180°C). Line an 8-inch (20-cm) square baking dish with aluminum foil.

To make the pastry, sift together the flour, cornstarch and salt into a bowl; set aside. Combine the butter, sugar and lemon zest in a large bowl. Using an electric mixer set on high speed, beat until light and fluffy. Reduce the speed to low, add the flour mixture and mix until the ingredients begin to gather together into a dough. Turn out onto a large sheet of waxed paper and pat into a square. Cover with a second sheet of waxed paper. Roll out the dough into a square ¼ inch (6 mm) thick. Refrigerate for 10 minutes.

Transfer the pastry to the prepared dish, trimming it so the sides are 1 inch (2.5 cm) high. Pierce all over with a fork. Bake until beginning to color, about 35 minutes. Remove from the oven. Leave the oven set at 350°F (180°C).

To make the topping, combine the butter, brown sugar and honey in a heavy saucepan. Whisk over medium-high heat and bring to a boil. Boil without whisking until thickened and the bubbles enlarge, about 1 minute. Stir in the nuts. Remove from the heat and stir in the cream. Spread the topping in the crust.

Bake until the caramel bubbles, about 20 minutes. Let cool in the dish on a wire rack.

Using the foil lift the sheet from the dish. Peel back the foil sides. Cut into 1½-inch (4-cm) squares. Store refrigerated in an airtight container for up to 5 days.

Makes about 2 dozen

S'More Bars

FOR THE CRUST:

5 whole graham crackers

¾ cup (4 oz/125 g) all-purpose (plain) flour

½ cup (3½ oz/105 g) firmly packed golden brown sugar

½ cup (¼ lb/125 g) unsalted butter, chilled, cut into ½-inch (12-mm) pieces

1 egg, lightly beaten

FOR THE TOPPING:

6 tablespoons (3 fl oz/80 ml) heavy (double) cream

9 oz (280 g) milk chocolate, chopped

1 cup (2 oz/60 g) miniature marshmallows

The ritual campfire combination of graham cracker, chocolate and marshmallow is re-created in an unforgettable cookie. Great by a campfire or at home by the fireplace on a chilly night.

✳

Preheat an oven to 350°F (180°C). Line an 8-inch (20-cm) square baking pan with aluminum foil.

To make the crust, crumble the graham crackers into a food processor fitted with the metal blade. Process finely. Add the flour and brown sugar and process to mix. Add the butter and process until the mixture resembles fine meal. Add the egg and process only until the mixture is evenly moist. Transfer the mixture to the prepared pan and press into the bottom to form a crust.

Bake until the top is just firm to the touch, about 20 minutes. Let cool completely in the pan on a wire rack.

To make the topping, place the cream in a heavy saucepan and bring to a simmer. Remove from the heat. Add the chocolate and stir until melted and smooth. Mix in the marshmallows. Spread the chocolate mixture evenly over the cooled crust. Cover and refrigerate until firm, at least 2 hours.

Using the foil lift the sheet from the pan. Peel back the foil sides. Cut into bars 2 inches (5 cm) by 1¼ inches (3 cm). Remove the bars from the foil. Store in an airtight container in the refrigerator for up to 5 days.

Makes about 2 dozen

Cappuccino-Walnut Brownies

Instant coffee powder is the secret to the intense flavor here. The chocolate glaze is optional.

❋

FOR THE BROWNIES:

4 oz (125 g) unsweetened chocolate, chopped

6 tablespoons (3 oz/90 g) unsalted butter

2 teaspoons instant coffee powder

½ cup (2½ oz/75 g) all-purpose (plain) flour

¾ teaspoon ground cinnamon

¼ teaspoon salt

2 eggs

1½ cups (10½ oz/330 g) firmly packed brown sugar

1 cup (4 oz/125 g) walnut pieces

FOR THE GLAZE:

3 oz (90 g) semisweet chocolate, chopped

6 tablespoons (3 oz/90 g) unsalted butter

1 teaspoon instant coffee powder

½ heaping teaspoon ground cinnamon

*P*reheat an oven to 350°F (180°C). Line a 9-inch (23-cm) square pan or 7-by-11-inch (18-by-28-cm) baking dish with aluminum foil. Butter the foil, then dust with flour.

To make the brownies, combine the chocolate, butter and coffee powder in a small, heavy saucepan. Stir over low heat until melted and smooth. Let cool slightly.

Sift together the flour, cinnamon and salt into a bowl; set aside. In a large bowl whisk the eggs until foamy. Whisk in the brown sugar and then the chocolate mixture. Mix in the flour mixture just until blended. Fold in the walnuts. Spread the batter in the prepared pan.

Bake until just springy to the touch and a toothpick inserted in the center comes out with a few crumbs attached, about 40 minutes. Let cool in the pan on a wire rack.

To make the glaze, combine the chocolate, butter, coffee powder and cinnamon in the top pan of a double boiler over simmering water. Stir until melted and smooth. Alternatively, melt the ingredients together in a heatproof bowl placed over (not touching) gently simmering water. Chill, stirring occasionally, until just spreadable but not set, about 15 minutes. Spread the glaze on the cooled brownies. Let stand until set, about 15 minutes. Using the foil lift the sheet of brownies from the pan. Peel back the foil sides. Cut into 25 squares or diamonds. Wrap individually in plastic wrap and store in the refrigerator for up to 3 days.

Makes 25

Coconut, Almond and Chicolate Bars

Preheat an oven to 350°F (180°C). Line an 8-inch (20-cm) square baking pan with aluminum foil. Butter the foil.

To make the crust, combine the flour, brown sugar and salt in a food processor fitted with the metal blade. Process to mix well. Add the butter and almonds and process until the texture of a fine meal. Transfer the mixture to the prepared pan and press firmly into the bottom to form a crust.

Bake until the crust is barely firm to the touch, about 40 minutes. Let cool completely in the pan on a wire rack.

Meanwhile, to make the filling, place the cream of coconut in a small, heavy saucepan and bring to a simmer. Reduce the heat to low. Add the white chocolate and stir until melted. Transfer to a bowl. Add the sour cream and butter and mix until melted and smooth. Stir in the coconut. Cover and refrigerate for 1 hour, stirring occasionally. Spoon the filling into the cooled crust; smooth the top. Refrigerate while preparing the topping.

To make the topping, in a small, heavy saucepan bring the cream and butter to a simmer, stirring frequently. Reduce to low, add the chocolate and stir to melt. Pour the hot topping over the filling. Using a small icing spatula or the back of a spoon, spread to cover evenly; shake the pan from side to side to smooth the surface. Cover and refrigerate overnight.

Using the foil lift the sheet from the pan. Cut into bars 1½ inches (4 cm) by ¾ inch (2 cm). Store refrigerated in an airtight container for up to 5 days.

Makes about 3½ dozen

FOR THE CRUST:

1 cup (5 oz/155 g) all-purpose (plain) flour

¼ cup (2 oz/60 g) firmly packed dark brown sugar

¼ teaspoon salt

6 tablespoons (3 oz/90 g) unsalted butter, chilled, cut into ½-inch (12-mm) pieces

¾ cup (3½ oz/105 g) slivered blanched almonds, toasted and chopped

FOR THE FILLING:

½ cup (4 fl oz/125 ml) well-stirred canned cream of coconut

3 oz (90 g) imported white chocolate, chopped

¼ cup (2 fl oz/60 ml) sour cream

¼ cup (2 oz/60 g) unsalted butter, at room temperature

1¼ cups (3½ oz/105 g) lightly packed sweetened flaked coconut

FOR THE TOPPING:

3 tablespoons heavy (double) cream

3 tablespoons unsalted butter

3½ oz (105 g) semisweet chocolate, chopped

Chocolate-Cranberry Bars

FOR THE CRUST:

1 cup (3 oz/90 g) old-fashioned rolled
    oats or quick-cooking oats

½ cup (3½ oz/105 g) firmly packed dark
    brown sugar

⅓ cup (2 oz/60 g) all-purpose (plain)
    flour

¼ teaspoon baking soda (bicarbonate
    of soda)

⅛ teaspoon salt

⅓ cup (3 oz/90 g) unsalted butter,
    melted

FOR THE TOPPING:

½ cup (¼ lb/125 g) unsalted butter

2 oz (60 g) unsweetened chocolate,
    chopped

1 teaspoon instant espresso powder

2 eggs

1 cup (8 oz/250 g) granulated sugar

¼ cup (1½ oz/45 g) all-purpose (plain)
    flour

2 teaspoons vanilla extract (essence)

⅛ teaspoon salt

½ cup (2 oz/60 g) dried cranberries

*Dried cranberries add a touch of tartness to the chocolate topping;
chopped dried apricots or sour cherries can be used instead. Cut
these rich treats into small bars, then pack them for a picnic or hike.*

❊

*P*reheat an oven to 350°F (180°C). Line an 8-inch (20-cm)
square baking pan with foil. Butter the foil.

To make the crust, stir together the oats, brown sugar,
flour, baking soda and salt in a bowl. Add the melted butter
and mix until crumbly. Transfer the mixture to the prepared
pan and press firmly into the bottom to form a crust. Bake
for 10 minutes.

Meanwhile, to make the topping, combine the butter,
chocolate and espresso powder in a heavy saucepan over low
heat. Stir until melted and smooth. Remove from the heat.

Combine the eggs, sugar, flour, vanilla and salt in a bowl
and whisk until well mixed. Whisk in the chocolate mixture
and cranberries.

When the crust is ready, pour the filling over the hot crust.
Continue to bake until the edges are set but the center is still
soft although not liquid, about 40 minutes longer. Let cool
in the pan on a wire rack.

Using the foil lift the cooled sheet from the pan and place
on a work surface. Peel back the foil sides. Cut into bars
2½ inches (6 cm) by 1½ inches (4 cm). Remove the bars
from the foil. Wrap individually in plastic wrap and store at
room temperature for up to 3 days.

Makes about 15

Peanut and Milk Chocolate Chip Cookies

2¼ cups (11½ oz/360 g) all-purpose (plain) flour
1 teaspoon baking soda (bicarbonate of soda)
½ teaspoon salt
1 cup (½ lb/250 g) unsalted butter, at room temperature
¾ cup (6 oz/185 g) granulated sugar
¾ cup (6 oz/185 g) firmly packed dark brown sugar
2 teaspoons vanilla extract (essence)
2 eggs
1½ cups (9 oz/280 g) milk chocolate chips
1½ cups (7 oz/220 g) coarsely chopped lightly salted dry-roasted peanuts

This combination of flavors seems to be a favorite with everyone, and so do these cookies—especially as after-work or after-school snacks. To make 12 giant cookies, divide the dough into 12 pieces and bake as directed.

✢

Preheat an oven to 350°F (180°C).

Sift together the flour, baking soda and salt into a bowl; set aside. Combine the butter, granulated sugar, brown sugar and vanilla in a large bowl. Using an electric mixer set on high speed, beat until light and fluffy. Add the eggs and beat well. Reduce the speed to low, add the flour mixture and mix until well blended. Mix in the chocolate chips and peanuts on low speed.

Drop the dough by rounded tablespoons onto ungreased baking sheets, spacing 2 inches (5 cm) apart. Bake until just beginning to brown around the edges, about 25 minutes. Transfer the cookies to wire racks to cool. Store in an airtight container at room temperature for up to 4 days.

Makes about 3 dozen

Chocolate Chip–Pecan Cookies

1¼ cups (6½ oz/200 g) all-purpose (plain) flour

½ teaspoon baking soda (bicarbonate of soda)

⅛ teaspoon salt

½ cup (¼ lb/125 g) unsalted butter, at room temperature

¾ cup (6 oz/185 g) firmly packed brown sugar

1 teaspoon vanilla extract (essence)

1 egg

1½ cups (9 oz/280 g) semisweet chocolate chips

1½ cups (6 oz/185 g) chopped pecans

The recipe calls for twice as many chips and nuts as usual. Drizzle with chocolate coating or caramel glaze (recipes on page 12) to put these chunky treats over the top.

❖

*P*reheat an oven to 375°F (190°C).

Sift together the flour, baking soda and salt into a bowl; set aside. Combine the butter, brown sugar and vanilla in a large bowl. Using an electric mixer set on high speed, beat until light and fluffy. Beat in the egg. Reduce the speed to low, add the flour mixture and mix just until incorporated. Mix in the chocolate chips and pecans on low speed.

Spoon the batter by rounded tablespoons onto ungreased baking sheets, spacing 2 inches (5 cm) apart. Bake until just firm to the touch and beginning to brown, about 15 minutes. Transfer the cookies to wire racks to cool. Store in an airtight container at room temperature for up to 4 days.

Makes about 2 dozen

Oatmeal, Date and Walnut Cookies

2 cups (10 oz/315 g) all-purpose (plain) flour

1 tablespoon ground cinnamon

1 teaspoon baking soda (bicarbonate of soda)

1 teaspoon salt

¾ cup (6 oz/185 g) unsalted butter, at room temperature

1 cup (8 oz/250 g) granulated sugar

1 cup (7 oz/220 g) firmly packed dark brown sugar

2 whole eggs

1 egg yolk

3 tablespoons milk

2 teaspoons vanilla extract (essence)

2½ cups (7½ oz/235 g) old-fashioned rolled oats or quick-cooking oats

½ lb (250 g) dates, chopped (about 1½ cups)

2 cups (8 oz/250 g) walnuts, coarsely chopped

A great recipe for a big batch of long-keeping, old-fashioned cookies. You can alter the baking time according to your preference for chewy or crisp cookies.

✣

Preheat an oven to 375°F (190°C). Butter baking sheets.

Sift together the flour, cinnamon, baking soda and salt into a bowl; set aside. Place the butter in a large bowl. Using an electric mixer set on high speed, beat until light and fluffy. Beat in the granulated sugar and brown sugar. Add the whole eggs, egg yolk, milk and vanilla and beat until light and fluffy, about 2 minutes. Reduce the speed to low, add the flour mixture and mix just until incorporated. Mix in the oats, dates and walnuts on low speed.

Drop the batter by rounded tablespoons onto the prepared baking sheets, spacing 2 inches (5 cm) apart. Bake until light brown, about 12 minutes for chewy cookies and about 15 minutes for crisp cookies. Let cool on the baking sheets for 1 minute. Transfer the cookies to wire racks to cool completely. Store in an airtight container in the refrigerator for up to 1 week.

Makes about 4 dozen

Lemon and Currant Cookies

1 cup (5 oz/155 g) plus 3 tablespoons
   all-purpose (plain) flour

¾ teaspoon baking powder

⅛ teaspoon baking soda (bicarbonate
   of soda)

¼ teaspoon ground nutmeg

⅛ teaspoon salt

½ cup (¼ lb/125 g) plus 2 tablespoons
   unsalted butter, at room temperature

¾ cup (6 oz/185 g) granulated sugar

1 tablespoon fresh lemon juice

2¼ teaspoons grated lemon zest

1 teaspoon vanilla extract (essence)

1 egg

¾ cup (4½ oz/140 g) dried currants

confectioners' sugar icing, optional
   (recipe on page 13)

grated lemon zest, optional

A delicate cookie with lots of lemon flavor. Terrific coated with confectioners' sugar icing and sprinkled with grated lemon zest. For tiny cookies, use a rounded ½ teaspoon dough for each and bake for about 5 minutes.

✧

*P*reheat an oven to 350°F (180°C).

Sift together the flour, baking powder, baking soda, nutmeg and salt into a bowl; set aside. Combine the butter, sugar, lemon juice, the 2¼ teaspoons lemon zest and vanilla in a large bowl. Using an electric mixer set on high speed, beat until light and fluffy. Beat in the egg. Reduce the speed to low, add the flour mixture and mix just until incorporated. Mix in the currants on low speed.

Drop the batter by slightly rounded teaspoons onto ungreased baking sheets, spacing 2 inches (5 cm) apart. Bake until brown around the edges, about 10 minutes. Let cool on the baking sheets for 2 minutes. Transfer the cookies to wire racks to cool completely.

Spread the tops of the cooled cookies with confectioners' sugar icing and sprinkle with grated lemon zest, if desired. Store in an airtight container in the refrigerator for up to 5 days.

Makes about 2 dozen

Chocolate-Chunk and Cherry Cookies

1 cup (5 oz/155 g) all-purpose (plain) flour

¾ teaspoon baking powder

⅛ teaspoon baking soda (bicarbonate of soda)

⅛ teaspoon salt

½ cup (¼ lb/125 g) plus 2 tablespoons unsalted butter, at room temperature

¾ cup (6 oz/185 g) firmly packed dark brown sugar

1 teaspoon vanilla extract (essence)

1 egg

8 oz (250 g) semisweet chocolate, cut into ½-inch (12-mm) pieces (about 1½ cups)

6 oz (185 g) dried sour cherries, dried Bing cherries or dried cranberries, chopped (about 1½ cups)

Use big hunks of premium chocolate to make these chocolate-rich cookies extra special. Dried cherries or cranberries provide sophisticated flavor; if they're unavailable, raisins or currants can be substituted with excellent results.

❖

*P*reheat an oven to 350°F (180°C).

Sift together the flour, baking powder, baking soda and salt into a bowl; set aside. Combine the butter, brown sugar and vanilla in a large bowl. Using an electric mixer set on high speed, beat until fluffy. Beat in the egg. Reduce the speed to low, add the flour mixture and mix in just until incorporated. Mix in the chocolate and cherries or cranberries on low speed.

Drop the batter by slightly rounded tablespoons onto ungreased baking sheets, spacing 2 inches (5 cm) apart. Bake until golden brown, about 16 minutes. Transfer the cookies to wire racks to cool. Store in an airtight container at room temperature for up to 4 days.

Makes about 2 dozen

Caramel-Apple Oat Chews

1½ cups (4½ oz/140 g) old-fashioned
rolled oats

1½ cups (7½ oz/235 g) all-purpose
(plain) flour

¾ teaspoon baking soda (bicarbonate
of soda)

¼ teaspoon salt

½ cup (¼ lb/125 g) plus 2 tablespoons
unsalted butter, at room temperature

1 cup (7 oz/220 g) plus 2 tablespoons
firmly packed golden brown sugar

1 egg

2 tablespoons milk

¾ teaspoon vanilla extract (essence)

1 cup (4 oz/125 g) peeled, cored and
chopped apple

1 cup (6 oz/185 g) chopped dried apple

hot caramel glaze *(recipe on page 12)*

Perfect for kids' parties or lunch boxes. The caramel glaze makes them taste like caramel-coated apples.

✣

*P*reheat an oven to 350°F (180°C). Butter baking sheets.

Stir together the oats, flour, baking soda and salt in a bowl; set aside. Combine the butter and brown sugar in a large bowl. Using an electric mixer set on high speed, beat until light and fluffy. Add the egg, milk and vanilla and beat until very fluffy, about 2 minutes. Reduce the speed to low, add the oat-flour mixture and mix until well blended. Mix in the fresh and dried apples on low speed.

Drop the dough by rounded tablespoons onto the prepared baking sheets, spacing 2 inches (5 cm) apart. Bake until golden, about 15 minutes. Transfer the cookies to wire racks to cool completely.

Drizzle the cooled cookies with the hot caramel glaze. Store in an airtight container in the refrigerator for up to 4 days.

Makes about 2 dozen

Ginger-Almond Florentines

½ cup (4 fl oz/125 ml) plus 2 tablespoons heavy (double) cream
½ cup (4 oz/125 g) granulated sugar
¼ cup (2 oz/60 g) firmly packed dark
  brown sugar
2 tablespoons unsalted butter
⅔ cup (3 oz/90 g) sliced almonds,
  lightly toasted
¼ cup (1½ oz/45 g) all-purpose (plain)
  flour
¼ cup (½ oz/15 g) finely chopped
  crystallized ginger
2 teaspoons grated orange zest
1½ teaspoons grated lemon zest
½ recipe chocolate coating (recipe on
  page 12)

A light cookie to rival any you might purchase at a premium bakery. They keep for up to 2 weeks if layered between sheets of waxed paper and refrigerated in an airtight container.

❖

*P*reheat an oven to 350°F (180°C). Line 2 large, heavy baking sheets with aluminum foil. Lightly butter the foil.

Combine the cream, granulated sugar, brown sugar and butter in a heavy saucepan. Cook over medium heat, stirring constantly, just until the sugars dissolve and the butter melts. Add the almonds, flour, ginger, and orange and lemon zests. Bring the mixture to a boil, stirring constantly. Remove from the heat.

Drop 1 tablespoon batter (batter will be runny) onto a prepared baking sheet. Repeat five times, spacing cookies 3 inches (7.5 cm) apart. Repeat with the second baking sheet.

Bake until deep brown, about 10 minutes. Remove from the oven. Using a round cookie cutter or a glass 3 inches (7.5 cm) in diameter, push the hot cookie edges in toward the center to neaten them, shaping into 3-inch (7.5-cm) rounds. Slide the foil off the sheets. Line the same sheets with new foil, butter the foil and repeat with the remaining batter.

Cool the cookies completely on the foil. Carefully peel the cookies off the foil and arrange them smooth-side up on the baking sheets. Spoon 1 teaspoon of the hot chocolate coating in the center of each and, using a small icing spatula or knife, spread to the edges. Refrigerate until the chocolate is set, about 30 minutes. Store in an airtight container in the refrigerator for up to 2 weeks.

Makes about 2 dozen

Toasted-Almond Macaroons

1 cup (4½ oz/140 g) slivered blanched
   almonds, lightly toasted
⅔ cup (5 oz/155 g) granulated sugar
1 tablespoon all-purpose (plain) flour
1 egg white
1¼ teaspoons vanilla extract (essence)
¼ teaspoon almond extract (essence)
about 16 whole almonds

You must use the egg white from a large egg to achieve the correct consistency for the dough. If you happen to overbake these macaroons and they become a bit dry, place in an airtight container with an apple slice and let them sit overnight to soften.

🐚

Preheat an oven to 350°F (180°C). Line a baking sheet with aluminum foil.

Place the slivered almonds in a food processor fitted with the metal blade and process finely (do not process to a paste). Add the sugar and flour and process to a powder. Add the egg white, vanilla extract and almond extract and process until a wet paste forms.

Using damp hands, roll the dough between your palms to form 1-inch (2.5-cm) balls. Place on the prepared baking sheet, spacing 2 inches (5 cm) apart. Place a whole almond in the center of each.

Bake until just beginning to brown, about 10 minutes. Let cool on the baking sheet on a wire rack for 10 minutes. Gently peel off the foil and transfer the cookies to the rack to cool completely. Store in an airtight container at room temperature for up to 5 days.

Makes about 16

Ginger Cookie-Press Cookies

2 cups (10 oz/315 g) all-purpose (plain) flour

1½ teaspoons ground ginger

1 teaspoon ground cinnamon

¼ teaspoon ground cloves

¼ teaspoon salt

1 cup (½ lb/250 g) unsalted butter, at room temperature

¾ cup (6 oz/185 g) firmly packed golden brown sugar

1 tablespoon grated orange zest

With a cookie press, it's easy to turn out attractively shaped cookies in minutes. Formed into holiday patterns and decorated with colored crystal sugars or confectioners' sugar icing (recipe on page 13), they're just the thing for a special occasion.

Preheat an oven to 350°F (180°C).

Sift together the flour, ginger, cinnamon, cloves and salt into a bowl; set aside. Combine the butter, brown sugar and orange zest in a large bowl. Using an electric mixer set on high speed, beat until light and fluffy. Reduce the speed to low, add the flour mixture and mix until well blended.

Pack the dough into a cookie press. Fit with the desired design plate. Press the dough out onto ungreased baking sheets, spacing the cookies 1½ inches (4 cm) apart.

Bake until just firm to the touch, about 15 minutes. Transfer the cookies to wire racks to cool. Store in an airtight container at room temperature for up to 5 days.

Makes about 4 dozen

Walnut-Cardamom Viennese Crescents

1 cup (5 oz/155 g) all-purpose (plain) flour

¾ cup (3 oz/90 g) walnuts

½ cup (¼ lb/125 g) unsalted butter, chilled, cut into ½-inch (12-mm) pieces

¼ cup (2 oz/60 g) granulated sugar

1 teaspoon vanilla extract (essence)

½ teaspoon ground cardamom

½ teaspoon grated orange zest

pinch of salt

vanilla sugar (recipe on page 11) or confectioners' (icing) sugar

Using a food processor, it takes only minutes to get these into the oven. They can be made even faster if formed into 1-inch (2.5-cm) balls rather than crescent shapes.

❀

Preheat an oven to 325°F (165°C).

Combine all the ingredients except the vanilla sugar or confectioners' sugar in a food processor fitted with the metal blade. Using rapid off-on pulses, process until the mixture resembles coarse meal. Then process continuously until the dough begins to gather together.

Roll 2 teaspoons dough between your palms to form a rope 2½ inches (6 cm) long, slightly tapering it at the ends. Arrange the rope on an ungreased baking sheet in a crescent shape (see page 10). Repeat with the remaining dough, spacing the cookies 1 inch (2.5 cm) apart.

Bake until just firm to the touch, about 20 minutes. Let cool on the baking sheet for 5 minutes. Transfer the cookies to a wire rack. Sprinkle vanilla sugar over the warm cookies or sieve confectioners' sugar over cooled cookies. Store in an airtight container at room temperature for up to 5 days.

Makes about 2 dozen

Ginger Molasses Cookies

2 cups (10 oz/315 g) all-purpose (plain) flour

2 teaspoons baking soda (bicarbonate of soda)

2 teaspoons ground ginger

1½ teaspoons ground cinnamon

1 teaspoon ground cloves

1 teaspoon salt

½ cup (4 oz/125 g) vegetable shortening

¼ cup (2 oz/60 g) unsalted butter, at room temperature

1 cup (7 oz/220 g) firmly packed dark brown sugar

1 egg

¼ cup (2 fl oz/60 ml) dark molasses

2 teaspoons grated orange zest

granulated sugar

A New England classic. Keep a batch in the cookie jar for the perfect anytime snack.

Sift together the flour, baking soda, ginger, cinnamon, cloves and salt into a bowl; set aside. Combine the shortening, butter and brown sugar in a large bowl. Using an electric mixer set on high speed, beat until fluffy. Add the egg, molasses and orange zest and beat until blended. Reduce the speed to low, add the flour mixture and mix until just incorporated. Cover and refrigerate for 1 hour or as long as overnight.

Preheat an oven to 350°F (180°C). Lightly butter baking sheets.

Using wet hands, form the dough into 1¼-inch (3-cm) balls, then roll in granulated sugar to coat evenly. Arrange on the prepared baking sheets, spacing 2 inches (5 cm) apart.

Bake until pale golden and cracked on top but still soft, about 12 minutes. Let cool for 1 minute. Gently transfer the cookies to wire racks to cool. Store in an airtight container at room temperature for up to 1 week.

Makes about 2½ dozen

Peanut Butter Cup Cookies

FOR THE FILLING:

¾ cup (7 oz/220 g) creamy peanut
butter

3 tablespoons unsalted butter, at room
temperature

¾ teaspoon vanilla extract (essence)

½ cup (2 oz/60 g) confectioners' (icing)
sugar

FOR THE COOKIES:

1¾ cups (9 oz/280 g) all-purpose (plain)
flour

⅔ cup (2 oz/60 g) unsweetened cocoa,
preferably Dutch process

1 teaspoon baking soda (bicarbonate
of soda)

½ teaspoon baking powder

½ teaspoon salt

½ cup (4 oz/125 g) vegetable shortening,
at room temperature

6 tablespoons (3 oz/90 g) unsalted
butter, at room temperature

1 cup (8 oz/250 g) granulated sugar,
plus sugar for coating

1 egg

2 tablespoons milk

¼ teaspoon almond extract (essence)

*Thumbprint cookies that taste just like peanut butter cup candies,
only better. Try them as a snack with a glass of cold milk.*

❦

To make the filling, combine the peanut butter, butter and
vanilla in a food processor fitted with the metal blade.
Process until smooth. Blend in the confectioners' sugar.
Alternatively, place the first 3 ingredients in a bowl and beat
with an electric mixer set on medium speed until smooth.
On low speed mix in the sugar. Set aside.

Preheat an oven to 350°F (180°C). Butter baking sheets.
To make the cookies, sift together the flour, cocoa, baking
soda, baking powder and salt into a bowl; set aside.

Combine the shortening, butter and the 1 cup (8 oz/250 g)
sugar in a large bowl. Using an electric mixer set on high
speed, beat until light and fluffy. Add the egg, milk and
almond extract and beat until very fluffy, about 2 minutes. On
low speed mix in the flour mixture until just incorporated.

Using damp hands roll the dough between your palms to
form 1-inch (2.5-cm) balls. Roll the balls in sugar to coat
evenly. Place on the prepared baking sheets, spacing
2 inches (5 cm) apart. Using your thumb, make a large
indentation in the center of each.

Bake until puffed and slightly cracked, about 12 minutes.
Remove from the oven and mound about 1 teaspoon filling
in the center of each. Let cool for 1 minute, then transfer
to wire racks to cool completely. Store refrigerated in an
airtight container for up to 3 days.

Makes about 4 dozen

11 MARS 1993
Grèce :
le grand bleu
(Gallia, Jet Tours,
tugal, Locatour).
Portugatours

Honey and Orange Madeleines

melted butter and all-purpose (plain)
   flour for pan
2 eggs
⅓ cup (4 oz/125 g) honey
¼ cup (2 oz/60 g) granulated sugar
1½ teaspoons grated orange zest
⅛ teaspoon ground allspice
½ teaspoon vanilla extract (essence)
1 cup (4 oz/125 g) all-purpose (plain)
   flour, sifted before measuring
¾ cup (6 oz/185 g) unsalted butter,
   melted and cooled to lukewarm
plain granulated sugar or vanilla sugar
   (recipe on page 11)

The classic, fancifully shaped sponge-cake cookies are baked in a special pan that has shell-shaped indentations. Sifting the flour before measuring ensures the cookies have a light texture.

❀

*P*reheat an oven to 400°F (200°C). Generously brush a 12-mold madeleine pan with melted butter; dust with flour.

In a large bowl combine the eggs, honey, the ¼ cup (2 oz/60 g) sugar, orange zest and allspice. Set over a saucepan of simmering water (the water must not touch the bowl) and whisk just until lukewarm.

Transfer the bowl to a work surface and, using an electric mixer set on high speed, beat until pale yellow, light, foamy and tripled in volume, about 10 minutes. Beat in the vanilla. Reduce the speed to low and gradually mix in the flour.

Transfer one third of the batter to another bowl and gradually fold the melted butter into it (do not fold in the water that separates out at the bottom of the butter pan). Then gently fold the mixture into the remaining batter. Spoon into the prepared molds, filling almost to the top and using about half the batter.

Bake until golden brown and springy to the touch, about 12 minutes, rotating the pan 180 degrees halfway through baking. Immediately invert the pan onto a wire rack. Using a knife, gently pry out the cookies. Sprinkle with plain sugar or vanilla sugar. Wipe out the pan, brush with melted butter, dust with flour and repeat with the remaining batter. Let the cookies cool completely on the racks. Store in an airtight container at room temperature for up to 3 days.

Makes about 2 dozen

Chocolate-Peppermint Cookie-Press Cookies

¾ cup (6 oz/185 g) unsalted butter, at room temperature

¾ cup (6 oz/185 g) granulated sugar

1 egg

1½ teaspoons vanilla extract (essence)

1½ teaspoons peppermint extract (essence)

⅛ teaspoon salt

¼ cup (¾ oz/20 g) unsweetened cocoa, preferably Dutch process

1½ cups (7½ oz/235 g) all-purpose (plain) flour

For an added touch, finely chop peppermint candies or candy canes in a food processor, mix them with an equal amount of confectioners' (icing) sugar and coat the warm cookies by tossing them in the mixture.

Preheat an oven to 375°F (190°C).

Combine the butter and sugar in a large bowl. Using an electric mixer set on high speed, beat until light. Add the egg, vanilla, peppermint and salt and beat until light and fluffy. Reduce the speed to low, add the cocoa and mix in. Then add the flour and mix until well blended.

Pack the dough into a cookie press. Fit with the desired design plate. Press the dough out onto ungreased baking sheets, spacing the cookies 1 inch (2.5 cm) apart.

Bake until firm to the touch, about 10 minutes. Transfer the cookies to wire racks to cool. Store in an airtight container at room temperature for up to 5 days.

Makes about 4 dozen

Chocolate Chip, Currant and Cinnamon Rugelach

FOR THE PASTRY:
1 cup (½ lb/250 g) unsalted butter, at room temperature

½ lb (250 g) cream cheese, at room temperature

¼ teaspoon salt

2 cups (10 oz/315 g) all-purpose (plain) flour

FOR THE FILLING:
¼ cup (2 oz/60 g) unsalted butter, melted

¾ cup (6 oz/185 g) cinnamon sugar (*recipe on page 11*)

1⅓ cups (8 oz/250 g) miniature semisweet chocolate chips

1⅓ cups (8 oz/250 g) dried currants

FOR THE TOPPING:
1 egg white, beaten with 1 tablespoon water

¼ cup (2 oz/60 g) cinnamon sugar (*recipe on page 11*)

This is a delicious variation on a Jewish favorite.

To make the pastry, combine the butter and cream cheese in a large bowl. Using an electric mixer set on high speed, beat until smooth. Mix in the salt. Using a spoon add the flour and mix well. With floured hands, form the dough into a log. Cut into 4 equal pieces. Flatten each piece into a disk and wrap separately in waxed paper. Refrigerate overnight.

Preheat an oven to 375°F (190°C). Butter baking sheets. Let 1 dough disk stand at room temperature about 10 minutes to soften slightly. Place on a floured sheet of waxed paper, flour the disk and top with more waxed paper. Roll out to a round ⅛ inch (3 mm) thick. Loosen the paper and remove the top sheet.

To make the filling, brush the dough surface with 1 tablespoon melted butter. Immediately sprinkle with 3 tablespoons cinnamon sugar. Top with one-fourth of the chocolate chips and one-fourth of the currants. Using a rolling pin, gently roll over the filling to help adhere. Cut the round of dough into 12 wedges. Starting at the wide end, roll up each wedge. Transfer the cookies to a prepared baking sheet, arranging point-sides down and spacing 1 inch (2.5 cm) apart. Repeat with the remaining dough disks and filling ingredients.

For the topping, brush the cookies with the egg white–water mixture, then sprinkle with the cinnamon sugar. Bake until golden brown, about 15 minutes. Transfer to wire racks to cool. Store in an airtight container at room temperature for up to 5 days.

Makes 4 dozen

Vanilla Cookie-Press Ribbons

1 cup (½ lb/250 g) unsalted butter, at
  room temperature
1 cup (8 oz/250 g) granulated sugar
1 egg
2½ teaspoons vanilla extract (essence)
½ teaspoon ground cardamom
½ teaspoon salt
2½ cups (10 oz/315 g) all-purpose
  (plain) flour, sifted before measuring
vanilla sugar, optional (*recipe on page 11*)

A touch of cardamom adds an unusual accent to what is essentially a vanilla cookie. Use the ribbon-design plate in the cookie press to make festive, 4-inch (10-cm) ribbons. Be sure to use only a large egg for this recipe, to achieve a dough consistency that will extrude properly with the ribbon plate.

❀

Preheat an oven to 375°F (190°C).

Combine the butter and granulated sugar in a large bowl. Using an electric mixer set on high speed, beat until light and fluffy. Beat in the egg, vanilla extract, cardamom and salt. Using a spoon, stir in the flour until well mixed.

Pack the dough into a cookie press. Fit with the ribbon-design plate. Press the dough out onto ungreased baking sheets in strips 4 inches (10 cm) long.

Bake until golden brown, about 10 minutes. Gently transfer the cookies to wire racks. Sprinkle with vanilla sugar, if desired, and let cool. Store in an airtight container at room temperature for up to 4 days.

Makes about 3 dozen

Pecan Thumbprint Cookies

1 cup (5 oz/155 g) all-purpose (plain)
   flour
⅛ teaspoon salt
½ cup (¼ lb/125 g) unsalted butter, at
   room temperature
⅓ cup (2½ oz/75 g) firmly packed light
   brown sugar
¾ teaspoon vanilla extract (essence)
1 egg yolk
¾ cup (3 oz/90 g) pecans, coarsely
   ground
cinnamon sugar (recipe on page 11)
raspberry jam

Children find these irresistible. Filling half of the cookies with cinnamon sugar and half with raspberry jam adds an attractive contrast to the presentation.

❧

Preheat an oven to 350°F (180°C).

   Sift together the flour and salt into a small bowl; set aside. Combine the butter, brown sugar and vanilla in a large bowl. Using an electric mixer set on high speed, beat until light and fluffy. Mix in the egg yolk. Reduce the speed to low, add the flour mixture and pecans and mix just until incorporated.

   Roll pieces of the dough between your palms to form 1-inch (2.5-cm) balls. Arrange on an ungreased baking sheet, spacing 1½ inches (4 cm) apart. Using your thumb, make a depression about ¼ inch (6 mm) deep in the center of each ball. Fill the depression in half of the cookies with cinnamon sugar.

   Bake the cookies for 10 minutes. Fill the depressions in the unsugared cookies with jam. Continue baking the cookies until they begin to color, about 10 minutes longer. Transfer the cookies to wire racks to cool. Store in an airtight container at room temperature for up to 5 days.

Makes about 2 dozen

Maple-Walnut Rounds

1 cup (4 oz/125 g) walnuts

¾ cup (6 oz/185 g) firmly packed golden brown sugar

1 cup (½ lb/250 g) unsalted butter, at room temperature

1½ teaspoons maple extract (essence)

¼ teaspoon salt

2 cups (10 oz/315 g) all-purpose (plain) flour

about 3 dozen walnut halves

Flavored with maple extract, these cookies bring to mind the maple-walnut ice cream served in Vermont. Make a double batch and store them in a cookie jar.

❀

Preheat an oven to 350°F (180°C).

In a food processor fitted with the metal blade or in a blender, place the 1 cup (4 oz/125 g) walnuts and process coarsely. Add ¼ cup (2 oz/60 g) of the brown sugar and process finely; set aside.

Combine the butter, the remaining ½ cup (4 oz/125 g) brown sugar, maple extract and salt in a large bowl. Using an electric mixer set on high speed, beat until light and fluffy. Reduce the speed to low, add the flour and the nut mixture and mix until just incorporated.

Roll pieces of the dough between your palms to form 1-inch (2.5-cm) balls. Arrange on ungreased baking sheets, spacing 1½ inches (4 cm) apart. Press a walnut half into the center of each.

Bake the cookies until brown around the edges, about 20 minutes. Transfer the cookies to wire racks to cool. Store in an airtight container at room temperature for up to 5 days.

Makes about 3 dozen

Orange-Oatmeal Lace Cookies

¾ cup (6 oz/185 g) granulated sugar

¾ cup (2½ oz/75 g) firmly packed quick-cooking oats

¾ cup (4 oz/125 g) unbleached all-purpose (plain) flour

½ teaspoon baking powder

½ cup (¼ lb/125 g) plus 2 tablespoons unsalted butter, melted

¼ cup (2 fl oz/60 ml) milk

¼ cup (2 fl oz/60 ml) unsulfured light molasses

1 tablespoon grated orange zest

1 teaspoon vanilla extract (essence)

chocolate coating (*recipe on page 12*)

Fragile and sophisticated, these are perfect for an elegant tea or with coffee and fruit at the end of a dinner party. They're delicious plain, but even better when dipped in chocolate coating.

❧

*P*reheat an oven to 350°F (180°C). Line baking sheets with aluminum foil.

Combine the sugar, oats, flour and baking powder in a bowl. Add the melted butter, milk, molasses, orange zest and vanilla and stir until just blended. Let stand for 15 minutes.

Drop the batter onto the prepared baking sheets by heaping tablespoons, forming rounds 1 inch (2.5 cm) in diameter and spacing them 3 inches (7.5 cm) apart.

Bake until brown on the edges, about 10 minutes. Lift the foil with the cookies and transfer to a work surface. Let cool completely. Gently peel the cookies from the foil.

Line baking sheets with aluminum foil. Dip half of each cooled cookie into the hot chocolate coating. Place on the foil-lined baking sheets. Chill until the chocolate sets, about 20 minutes. Gently remove the cookies from the foil. Store in an airtight container in the refrigerator for up to 5 days.

Makes about 4 dozen

Pine-Nut Tassies

FOR THE PASTRY:

3 oz (90 g) cream cheese, at room
  temperature

½ cup (¼ lb/125 g) unsalted butter, at
  room temperature

1 cup (5 oz/155 g) all-purpose (plain)
  flour

FOR THE FILLING:

1 egg

¾ cup (6 oz/185 g) firmly packed dark
  brown sugar

1 tablespoon unsalted butter, at room
  temperature

1 teaspoon vanilla extract (essence)

pinch of salt

⅔ cup (3½ oz/105 g) pine nuts

*You'll need miniature muffin tins to make these tiny, sweet,
tartlike cookies, which are reminiscent of pecan pies. Great with
a cup of espresso.*

To make the pastry, combine the cream cheese and butter
in a bowl. Using an electric mixer set on high speed, beat
until well blended. Reduce the speed to low, add the flour
and mix until just incorporated.

Divide the dough between 2 large sheets of waxed paper.
Using the paper as an aid, form each portion into a log
6 inches (15 cm) long. Wrap each log in the paper and
refrigerate until firm, at least 1 hour or as long as overnight.

Preheat an oven to 325°F (165°C). Unwrap the dough and
cut each log into 12 rounds ½ inch (12 mm) thick. Press
each round into the bottom and up the sides of a miniature
muffin cup that is 1¾ inches (4.5 cm) in diameter; build the
edges up slightly beyond the rim.

To make the filling, combine the egg, brown sugar, butter,
vanilla and salt in a medium bowl and, using a spoon, mix
until smooth. Mix in half of the pine nuts. Spoon the
mixture into the cups, filling almost to the tops. Use the
remaining pine nuts to top the cookies.

Bake until the filling is set and the crusts begin to color,
about 30 minutes. Let cool completely in the muffin tins on
wire racks, then remove from the tins. Store in an airtight
container in the refrigerator for up to 3 days.

Makes 2 dozen

Cinnamon-Poppy Sugar Twists

plain granulated sugar

1 sheet frozen puff pastry, about 9 oz (280 g), thawed

1 egg, beaten with 1 teaspoon milk

3 tablespoons cinnamon sugar (recipe on page 11)

1 teaspoon grated lemon zest

2 teaspoons poppyseeds

Particularly easy to make. Just cut and twist them out of purchased puff pastry. They're excellent with a cup of tea or a glass of milk.

❀

*P*osition a rack in the center of an oven and preheat the oven to 350°F (180°C).

Sprinkle a work surface generously with granulated sugar. Place the sheet of pastry atop the sugar and roll it out until it is ⅛ inch (3 mm) thick. Brush evenly with the egg-milk mixture. In a small bowl stir together the cinnamon sugar and lemon zest. Sprinkle evenly over the pastry. Then sprinkle with the poppyseeds.

Cut the pastry crosswise into long strips 1 inch (2.5 cm) wide. Pick up each pastry strip, twist it several times and place on an ungreased heavy baking sheet, pressing the ends onto the sheet to prevent untwisting (see page 10).

Bake until golden brown and crisp, about 20 minutes. Immediately transfer the cookies to wire racks to cool. Store in an airtight container at room temperature for up to 3 days.

Makes about 14

Glossary

The following glossary defines terms specifically as they relate to cookies and their preparation. Included are major and unusual ingredients, as well as basic techniques used in cookie making.

ALLSPICE
Sweet spice of Caribbean origin with a flavor suggesting a blend of **cinnamon, cloves** and **nutmeg,** hence its name. May be purchased as whole dried berries (below) or, for easy incorporation into cookie doughs or batters, ground.

ANISEEDS
Sweet licorice-flavored spice of Mediterranean origin, the small crescent-shaped seeds of a plant related to parsley. Generally sold as whole seeds, which may be crushed with a mortar and pestle.

BAKING POWDER
Commercial baking product combining three ingredients: **baking soda,** the source of the carbon-dioxide gas that causes cookie batters or doughs to rise; an acid, such as cream of tartar, calcium acid phosphate or sodium aluminum sulphate, which, when the powder is combined with a liquid, causes the baking soda to release its gas; and a starch such as **cornstarch** or **flour,** to keep the powder from absorbing moisture.

BAKING SODA
Also known as bicarbonate of soda or sodium bicarbonate, the active component of **baking powder** and the source of the carbon dioxide gas that leavens batters and doughs. Often used on its own when acidic ingredients such as buttermilk, yogurt or citrus juices are present.

BISCOTTI
Italian term, literally "twice-cooked," used for crisp cookies that are first baked in loaf form, then sliced and baked again.

CARDAMOM
Sweet, exotic-tasting spice (below) mainly used in Middle Eastern and Indian cooking and in Scandinavian baking. Its small seeds, which come enclosed inside a long husklike pod, are best purchased whole, then ground with a spice grinder or with a mortar and pestle as needed.

CINNAMON
Popular sweet spice for flavoring baked goods. The aromatic bark of a type of evergreen tree, it is sold as whole dried strips—cinnamon sticks—or, for easy incorporation into cookie doughs or batters, ground.

CLOVES
Rich and aromatic East African spice used whole or in its ground form to flavor both sweet and savory recipes.

COCOA
See Chocolate.

COCONUT
For baking purposes, shredded or flaked coconut is sold ready-to-use in cans or plastic packages in the baking section of most food stores. The label indicates

CHOCOLATE
When making cookies, purchase the best-quality chocolate you can find—unsweetened, bittersweet, semisweet or sweet, as the recipe requires.

Unsweetened Chocolate
Pure cocoa liquor (half cocoa butter and half chocolate solids) ground and solidified in block-shaped molds. Unpalatable to some when eaten on its own, it provides intense chocolate flavor when combined with sugar and butter, milk or cream in recipes. Also known as bitter chocolate.

Bittersweet Chocolate
Lightly sweetened eating or baking chocolate enriched with extra cocoa butter, which generally accounts for approximately 40 percent of its weight. Look for bittersweet chocolate that contains at least 50 percent.

Semisweet Chocolate
Eating or baking chocolate that is usually—but not always—slightly sweeter than bittersweet chocolate, which may be substituted.

Milk Chocolate
Primarily an eating chocolate, enriched with milk powder—the equivalent of up to 1 cup (8 fl oz/250 ml) whole milk in the average-sized bar.

White Chocolate
A chocolatelike product for eating or baking, made by combining pure cocoa butter with sugar, powdered milk and sometimes vanilla. Check labels to make sure that the white chocolate you buy is made exclusively with cocoa butter, without the addition of coconut oil or vegetable shortening.

Chocolate Chips
Any of several kinds of chocolate—usually semisweet, bittersweet, milk or white—molded into small drop shapes, for uniform incorporation into cookie doughs.

Unsweetened Cocoa
Richly flavored, fine-textured powder ground from the solids left after much of the cocoa butter has been extracted from chocolate liquor. Cocoa powder specially treated to reduce its natural acidity, resulting in a darker color and more mellow flavor, is known as Dutch process cocoa.

To Chop Chocolate
While a food processor fitted with the metal blade can be used, a sharp, heavy knife offers better control.

First, break the chocolate by hand into small chunks, handling it as little as possible to avoid melting. Then, using a heavy knife and a clean, dry, odor-free chopping surface, carefully chop into smaller pieces.

Steadying the knife tip with your hand, continue chopping across the pieces until the desired consistency is reached.

whether the product is sweetened or unsweetened; most cookie recipes call for sweetened coconut. Canned sweetened cream of coconut, a rich concentrate of the fruit's liquid and fat, is also readily available in the baking or liquor section. Be sure to purchase coconut products from a store with a rapid turnover, to ensure freshness. Some recipes call for toasting flaked coconut to develop its flavor: Spread the flakes evenly on a baking sheet and bake in a 350°F (180°C) oven, stirring occasionally, until pale gold, 10–20 minutes.

CORNSTARCH
Fine, powdery flour ground from the endosperm of corn—the white heart of the kernel—and, because it contains no gluten, used to give a delicate texture to cookies and other baked goods. Also known as cornflour.

CREAM CHEESE
Smooth, white, mild-tasting cheese made from cream and milk, used on its own as a spread or as an ingredient that adds rich flavor and texture to baked goods and desserts. If possible, purchase cream cheese in bulk at good-quality delicatessens for better taste and a creamier texture.

Some recipes call for cream cheese that is at room temperature, to ease its blending with other ingredients. To achieve the correct temperature quickly, cut the cheese into ½-inch (12-mm) pieces and process briefly in a food processor fitted with the metal blade.

Alternatively, if the cheese is enclosed in an airtight commercial wrapper, leave the cheese in its wrapper and immerse it in a bowl of hot water until the desired consistency is reached, 2–3 minutes.

CREAM, HEAVY
Whipping cream with a butterfat content of at least 36 percent. For the best flavor and cooking properties, purchase only fresh cream with a short shelf life; avoid long-lasting varieties that have been processed by ultraheat methods. In Britain, use double cream.

DRIED FRUIT
Intensely flavored and satisfyingly chewy, many forms of sun-dried or kiln-dried fruits may be added to enhance the taste and/or texture of cookies. Select more recently dried and packaged fruits, which have a softer texture than older dried fruits. Usually found in specialty-food shops or the baking sections of food stores. Some of the most popular options include apples, apricots, cherries, cranberries, currants, dates, figs and pears.

Dried Pears

Currants

ESPRESSO POWDER, INSTANT
The strong, full flavor of espresso-roast coffee beans provides a distinctive source of flavor for cookie recipes. For an easily blended source of this intense flavor, use instant espresso powder or granules, found in the coffee section of food stores, in Italian delicatessens or in specialty coffee stores.

EGGS
Eggs are sold in the United States in a range of standard sizes, the most common being jumbo, extra large, large and medium. For the recipes in this book, use large eggs.

Separating Eggs
To separate an egg, crack the shell in half by tapping it against the side of a bowl and then breaking it apart with your fingers. Holding the shell halves over the bowl, gently transfer the whole yolk back and forth between them, letting the clear white drop away into the bowl. Take care not to cut into the yolk with the edges of the shell. Transfer the yolk to another bowl.

Alternatively, gently pour the egg from the shell onto the slightly cupped fingers of your outstretched (clean) hand, held over a bowl. Let the whites flow between your fingers into the bowl; the whole yolk will remain in your hand.

The same basic function is also performed by an aluminum, ceramic or plastic egg separator placed over a small bowl. The separator holds the yolk in its cuplike center while allowing the white to drip through slots in its sides.

EXTRACTS
Flavorings derived by dissolving essential oils of richly flavored foods—almonds, maple syrup, peppermint, vanilla—in an alcohol base. Use only products labeled "pure" or "natural" extract (essence).

FLOUR
The most common flour for making cookies is all-purpose flour (also called plain flour), a blend of hard and soft wheats available in all food markets. All-purpose flour is sold in its natural, pale yellow unbleached form or bleached, the result of a chemical process that not only whitens it but also makes it easier to blend with higher percentages of fat and sugar. Bleached flour is therefore commonly used for recipes where more tender results are desired, while unbleached flour yields more crisp results.

GINGER
The rhizome of the tropical ginger plant, which yields a sweet, strong-flavored spice. Ginger pieces are available crystallized or candied in specialty-food shops or the baking or Asian food section of food stores. Ground dried ginger is easily found in the spice section.

GRAHAM CRACKERS
Crisp, sweet crackers made from whole-wheat flour and usually **honey.** Cookies in their own right, they are sometimes crumbled or crushed for use as an ingredient in other dessert recipes.

NUTS

A wide variety of nuts complements cookie recipes. For the best selection, look in a specialty-food shop, health-food store or the baking section of a food market. Some of the most popular options include:

Almonds

Mellow, sweet nuts (below) that are an important crop in California and are popular throughout the world.

Cashews

Kidney-shaped, crisp nuts with a slightly sweet, buttery flavor. Native to tropical America but grown throughout the world, primarily in India.

Hazelnuts

Small, usually spherical nuts (below) with a slightly sweet flavor. Grown in Italy, Spain and the United States. Also known as filberts.

Macadamias

Spherical nuts (below), about twice the diameter of hazelnuts, with a very rich, buttery flavor and crisp texture. Native to Australia, they are now grown primarily in Hawaii.

Peanuts

When roasted, peanuts have a rich, full flavor and satisfying crispness that make them the world's most popular nut. So-called dry-roasted nuts are prepared in the dry heat of an oven rather than with the use of oil. The Virginia variety is longer and more oval than the smaller, rounder, red-skinned Spanish peanut.

Pecans

Brown-skinned, crinkly textured nuts (below) with a distinctive sweet, rich flavor and crisp, slightly crumbly texture. Native to the southern United States.

Pine Nuts

Small, ivory seeds (below) extracted from the cones of a species of pine tree, with a rich, slightly resinous flavor.

Pistachios

Slightly sweet, full-flavored nuts (below) with distinctively green, crunchy meat. Native to Asia Minor, they are grown primarily in the Middle East and California.

Walnuts

Rich, crisp-textured nuts with crinkled surfaces (right). English walnuts, the most familiar variety, are grown worldwide, although the largest crops are in California.

American black walnuts, sold primarily as shelled pieces, have a stronger flavor that lends extra distinction to desserts and candies.

To Blanch Nuts

Some nuts, such as almonds, can be blanched to loosen their papery skin. To blanch nuts, put them in a pan of boiling water for about 2 minutes; then drain and, when they are cool enough to handle, squeeze each nut between your fingers to slip it from its skin.

To Toast Nuts

Toasting brings out the full flavor and aroma of nuts. To toast any kind of nut, preheat an oven to 325°F (165°C). Spread the nuts in a single layer on a baking sheet and toast in the oven until they just begin to change color, 5–10 minutes. Remove from the oven and let cool to room temperature.

Toasting also loosens the skins of some nuts such as hazelnuts and walnuts, which may be removed by wrapping the still-warm nuts in a cotton towel and rubbing against them with the palms of your hands.

To Grind Nuts

A nut mill, which attaches to a countertop, is the best tool for grinding nuts evenly. Place the shelled nuts in the top compartment, called a hopper, and turn the hand crank. Some mills come with both small and medium cutting teeth.

Alternatively, a mortar and pestle or a food processor can be used. (If the nuts are to be ground into a flour, use a nut mill to achieve the proper texture.) When using a food processor, be careful not to process the nuts too long or their oils will be released and the nuts will turn into a paste.

HONEY

The natural, sweet, syruplike substance produced by bees from flower nectar, honey subtly reflects the color, taste and aroma of the blossoms from which it was made. Milder varieties, such as clover and orange blossom, are lighter in color and better suited to general cooking purposes. Provides a distinctive mellow sweetness in cookie recipes.

MAPLE SYRUP

Syrup made from boiling the sap of the maple tree, with an inimitably rich savor and intense sweetness. Buy maple syrup that is labeled "pure," rather than a blend.

MARSHMALLOWS

Fluffy candies made from beaten egg whites, gelatin and sugar syrup. Widely available in the baking or candy sections of food stores.

MOLASSES

Thick, robust-tasting, syrupy sugarcane by-product of sugar refining. Light "unsulfured" molasses results from the first boiling of the syrup; dark molasses from the second boiling.

NUTMEG

Popular baking spice that is the hard pit of the fruit of the nutmeg tree. May be bought already ground or, for fresher flavor, whole, to be ground on a nutmeg grater as needed.

OATS

Coarse-, medium- or fine-textured cereal (below) ground from hulled oats, prized for its nutlike taste and texture when cooked as a breakfast porridge or added to baked goods. For baking, use regular (old-fashioned) rolled oats—not quick-cooking or instant—unless otherwise specified.

POPPYSEEDS

Small, spherical, blue-black seeds of a form of poppy; traditionally used in central and Eastern European cooking to add rich, nutlike flavor to baked goods.

PUFF PASTRY

Form of pastry in which pastry dough and butter or some other solid fat are repeatedly layered to form thin leaves that puff up to flaky lightness when baked. Commercially manufactured frozen puff pastry, ready to defrost, roll, cut and bake, is available in food stores.

SHORTENING, VEGETABLE

Solid vegetable fat sometimes used in place of or in combination with butter in cookie doughs. The fat is said to "shorten" the flour, that is, to make it flaky and tender.

SUGAR

Many different forms of sugar are used to sweeten and decorate cookies.
Brown Sugar: A rich-tasting, fine-textured granulated sugar combined with **molasses** in varying quantities to yield golden, light or dark brown sugar. Widely available in the baking section of food stores.

Granulated Sugar: The standard, widely used form of pure white sugar. Do not use superfine granulated sugar unless specified.
Colored Sugar Crystals: Relatively large crystals of sugar colored with natural vegetable dyes and sprinkled onto finished baked goods for decoration.
Confectioners' Sugar: Finely pulverized sugar, also known as powdered or icing sugar, which dissolves quickly and provides a thin, white decorative coating. To prevent confectioners' sugar from absorbing moisture in the air and caking, manufacturers often mix a little **cornstarch** into it.

TOFFEE

Traditional English candy made from a sugar syrup, usually lightly caramelized, enriched with a generous amount of butter. Toasted almonds are often added to the mixture. Handmade or imported toffee can be found in specialty-food stores and candy shops; the most widely available, best-quality commercial U.S. brands are Heath Bar and Almond Roca.

VANILLA

Vanilla beans are dried aromatic pods of a variety of orchid; one of the most popular flavorings in dessert making. Vanilla is most commonly used in the form of an alcohol-based extract (essence); be sure to purchase products labeled "pure vanilla extract." Vanilla extract or beans from Madagascar are the best.

ZEST

Thin, brightly colored, outermost layer of a citrus fruit's peel, containing most of its aromatic essential oils— a lively source of flavor in baking. Zest may be removed using one of two easy methods:

1. Use a simple tool known as a zester, drawing its sharp-edged holes across the fruit's skin to remove the zest in thin strips. Alternatively, use a fine hand-held grater.

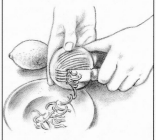

2. Holding the edge of a paring knife or vegetable peeler away from you and almost parallel to the fruit's skin, carefully cut off the zest in thin strips, taking care not to remove any white pith with it. Then thinly slice or chop on a cutting board.

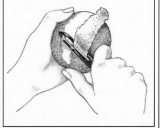

Index

✳

ACKNOWLEDGMENTS

The publishers would like to thank the following people and organizations for their generous assistance and support in producing this book:
William Garry, James Badham, Joel Liberson, Topanga Central, Sharon C. Lott, Stephen W. Griswold, Tara Brown, Ken DellaPenta,
the buyers for Gardener's Eden, and the buyers and store managers for Pottery Barn and Williams-Sonoma stores.

The following kindly lent props for the photography:
Biordi Art Imports, J. Goldsmith Antiques, Fillamento, Fredericksen Hardware, Forrest Jones, Stephanie Greenleigh, Sue Fisher King,
Lorraine & Judson Puckett, Waterford/Wedgwood, Sue White and Chuck Williams.